What People Are Saying About

Creating a Happy World

In a beautifully written and well-researched gem of a book, Patricia Saunders has opened a porthole through which we can see people's hopes for a happier life and a kinder world fulfilled. A must read for anyone who cares about the future of humanity.
Marci Shimoff, co-author, #1 *NY Times* bestseller, *Happy for No Reason* and *Chicken Soup for the Woman's Soul*

Creating a Happy World is a hugely important book for anyone who wants to experience more happiness. It not only brings to light a way to increase personal happiness regardless of the chaotic times we live in, but also how to generate increased well-being for society and make societal happiness, even global happiness, a permanent reality. This book could change your life, and all our lives, into something wonderful and extraordinary!
Bob Roth, bestselling author of *Strength in Stillness*

T0019559

Creating a Happy World

Cultivating Happiness through
the Transcendental Meditation® Program

Creating a Happy World

Cultivating Happiness through the Transcendental Meditation® Program

Patricia Anne Saunders

BOOKS

London, UK
Washington, DC, USA

CollectiveInk

First published by O-Books, 2024
O-Books is an imprint of Collective Ink Ltd.,
Unit 11, Shepperton House, 89 Shepperton Road, London, N1 3DF
office@collectiveinkbooks.com
www.collectiveinkbooks.com
www.o-books.com

For distributor details and how to order please visit the 'Ordering' section on our website.

Text copyright: Patricia Anne Saunders 2023

ISBN: 978 1 80341 522 2
978 1 80341 545 1 (ebook)
Library of Congress Control Number: 2023935540

A CIP catalogue record for this book is available from the British Library.

Design: Lapiz Digital Services

Printed and bound by CPI Group (UK) Ltd, Croydon, CR0 4YY
Printed in North America by CPI GPS partners

The author of this book does not dispense medical advice or prescribe the use of any technique as a form of treatment for physical, emotional, or medical problems without the advice of a physician, either directly or indirectly. The intent of the author is only to offer information of a general nature to help you in your quest for emotional and spiritual well-being. In the event you use any of the information in this book for yourself, which is your constitutional right, the author and the publisher assume no responsibility for your actions.

We operate a distinctive and ethical publishing philosophy in all areas of our business, from our global network of authors to production and worldwide distribution.

Also by Patricia Saunders

An Antidote to Violence: Evaluating the Evidence
ISBN: 978–1–78904–258–0

Contents

Acknowledgments

I would like to begin by thanking my excellent editors at O-Books, especially Elizabeth Radley, for recognizing the book's potential. I am also extremely grateful to Gerry Geer and Fran Clark for their thoughtful editing, encouragement, and assistance. They raised the book to a higher level than it would have been otherwise.

In addition, I cannot thank enough the many friends who offered encouragement and occasional help. So, many thanks to my husband; Douglas Carpenter for his untiring support; Fred Travis for sparking the theme in my mind; Park Hensley and Robert Herron for being the first people to read it through; Barry Spivack for suggesting a different arrangement of chapters; Margot Suettmann, Tara Schmid, and many others who encouraged me to finish the book.

My heartfelt appreciation also goes to the staff at John Hunt Publishing as their combined efforts helped to make this book what it is. Also, to all those who participated in research on the Transcendental Meditation program and took part in demonstrations of the Maharishi Effect; most of their names are unknown to me but I treasure them all the same.

Finally, I must express my sincere gratitude to Maharishi Mahesh Yogi and the Vedic tradition of knowledge, the source of the Transcendental Meditation program. Without Maharishi's understanding of consciousness and its practical application in society, *Creating a Happy World* would not have been written.

A big thank you to everyone. I have greatly appreciated your help and support.

Introduction

The great end of all human industry is the attainment of happiness. For this were arts invented, sciences cultivated, laws ordained, and societies modelled, by the most profound wisdom of patriots and legislators.

David Hume[1]

Human history over the past 5,000 years has been plagued with wars, famine, natural disasters, and climate change. With all the suffering and misery that these upheavals bring, it is hard to imagine a world where being happy is the norm. Happiness is the quality that makes life worth living and should be the natural birthright of everyone, but it seems this is not the case. Despite the many books giving advice on how to live a happier life, stress, worry, and sadness are on the rise, according to the 2022 World Happiness Report,[2] putting long-lasting happiness out of reach for many. Of course, the COVID-19 pandemic affected all of us, bringing with it lockdowns, isolated living, and the unpleasant long-term consequences of the illness, but COVID was not the only cause of the increase in sadness. Sadness has been quietly rising long before the World Happiness Report was first published.

Nowadays, we are at a crossroads in the search for happiness. On the one hand, we have material advantages undreamed of by our ancestors. We have heating and cooling systems, washer-dryers, fast means of travel, and even faster means of communication. On the other hand, we strive to understand how life can have meaning and whether the purpose of life is simply to survive. It is a confusing time, and in the middle of such confusion, something robust is needed to lift us out of the downward spiral of stress, sadness, and isolation. This is where *Creating a Happy World* can help.

1

Part I: Understanding Happiness

There are two paths to combat sadness and create a happy world. The first is the individual path, where happiness is considered in the light of personal circumstances, which may rotate between sadness and joy; and the second is transforming society to accelerate the experience of happiness for everyone. Thus, Part I of *Creating a Happy World* begins by looking at the different ways individuals achieve, or try to achieve, happiness. These range from the uncertain happiness of acquiring wealth and power, to reducing stress, developing friendships, the use and misuse of drugs, and eudaimonic behaviors (living what is considered a worthwhile life).

Given the transient nature of some of these routes, Part I takes the reader beyond the problems associated with finding happiness from the outside. Instead, it focuses on a solution that can enrich life from the inside; namely, the Transcendental Meditation technique, a simple, natural, effortless process practiced for 20 minutes twice a day without the need for a change of lifestyle or belief system. Everyone must, of course, be free to find their own way to inner happiness, but this book refers specifically to the Transcendental Meditation technique and its related programs for a very specific reason: it is the only meditation technique so far that published research has shown to positively improve both the quality of individual life and the quality of life for society. The term "quality of life" can, of course, include comfortable living conditions and a good working environment, but it must also include an increase in well-being, the composite term for happiness, life satisfaction, or emotional well-being, the overall fulfillment we can experience in everyday matters. Thus, an essential message of *Creating a Happy World* is that, with the program discussed in this book, well-being and fulfillment can be sustained, not just for a few days or weeks, but, with careful nurturing, for a very long time indeed.

Part II: Understanding Consciousness

There are many ways for human beings to develop, and Transcendental Meditation practice is one of these ways. It can enrich personal life, but it can also offer answers to universal questions such as: Who am I? Is the universe without ultimate meaning or purpose? Or is it dynamic with a very definite purpose? The answers to these questions are dependent on our ability to think and feel, our state of consciousness in fact, and how we understand consciousness. To put it bluntly, if consciousness did not exist, then neither would happiness, because happiness is bound up with consciousness. Thus, Part II examines the phenomenon of consciousness from the perspectives of three streams of philosophy: scientific materialism, dualism, and monism, all of which look for the truths of life and offer their own insights into the big questions. Part II explains how the insights of philosophy and neuroscience are based on the consciousness of the individual perceiver. It also discusses the different stages of human development, from the sensorimotor stage of babyhood to the highest states of consciousness that can be experienced in adulthood. In this light, *Creating a Happy World* explains that it is possible for human beings to experience an underlying state of inner silence, referred to as Transcendental Consciousness, the Self, the Tao, or Samādhi in the Yoga tradition—and on that basis, grow toward higher states of consciousness and the increasing happiness they bring.

Part III: Peace, the Basis of Happiness

Creating a Happy World holds that the expansion of very real and deep happiness is the purpose of life and, in Part III, examines the basis of happiness, which is peace, the foundation of tolerance and understanding even in a world of turmoil. But how many people can be happy living amid turmoil and conflict, sometimes violent conflict? Priorities change and desperation to survive is chief among them. Happiness becomes the fleeting joy of a kind word and, for some, the relief of living one more day. In the years to come, many who have endured conflict will suffer from insomnia, fear, grief, and extreme stress. There is not much happiness in a life such as this. Part III asks, therefore, whether a society, a nation, or even the world can arrive at a point where the majority of the population can feel happiness rather than sadness, and peace rather than turmoil.

Based on well-researched evidence, *Creating a Happy World* maintains that the conventional methods of peace-creation prevailing in the world today do not deal with the root cause of lack of peace. And if they do not deal with the root cause of conflict, then they do not deal with the root cause of unhappiness. In keeping with the premise that the experience of Transcendental Consciousness is profoundly peaceful and the source of human happiness, the book suggests a program that will increase our ability to experience peace, help those around us, and bring greater happiness even to distant people we cannot see. By the time readers have finished this book, the hope is that they will feel more happiness in their own lives, greater belief that life has a purpose, and increased optimism for the future of humanity. And lastly, a personal wish of mine is that *Creating a Happy World* will encourage more research into the connections between peace, happiness, and a contented world.

Part I

Understanding Happiness

Chapter 1

The Ideal and the Reality

राम राज दुख काहु न व्यापा
Rām Rāj dukh kāhu na vyāpā
In the reign of Rām suffering belonged to no one.

Rām Charit Mānasa[1]

The trees in the forest were ever full of flowers and fruit. The elephant and the lion dwelt peacefully together. Birds and deer forgot their animosities and lived in great harmony with one another. The cooing of the birds and the herds of deer fearlessly roaming the woods made a charming scene.

The air was cool, fragrant, and splendidly mild. Bees laden with honey made a pleasant humming. Creepers and trees yielded their sweetness on being asked. The earth was ever clothed with crops. Mines of jewels of every description were disclosed in the mountains, and the world acknowledged its king to be in truth the Universal Spirit.

Every river flowed with an abundance of refreshing water; cool, pure, and delicious to the taste. The sea remained within its bounds, casting forth pearls on its shore for men to gather. The ponds were thick with lotuses, and every quarter of the world was supremely happy.

The moon flooded the earth with her radiance; the sun gave as much heat as was necessary; the clouds poured forth showers for the mere asking in the days when Rām was king.

Rām Charit Mānasa[2]

The Rām Charit Mānasa (The lake of the deeds of Rāma) is a version of the Rāmāyana by the 16th century poet Goswāmi Tulsīdās. The Rāmāyana itself has been told and retold in a million different ways, yet the portrayal of happiness in this part of the text is not just beautiful poetry, but an inspiration for any human being, government, or society. The Rām Charit Mānasa presents the ideal of civilized life. It is grounded in the idea that human life is more than the synchronized functioning of biological or chemical parts, and that human beings can rise to heights of achievement and raise future generations to reach even the farthest stars. This may sound like an impossible dream that can only end in disappointment, yet every civilized society wants its people to be happy, healthy, and prosperous, living without war or conflict of any kind. Even if we believe the ideal cannot be reached, the idea of accepting the present state of life as the best we can do or abandoning ourselves to ever-increasing challenges, bureaucracy, and chaos cannot be the answer. Surely, it must be possible to create a happier and more satisfying world than we have at present.

Thomas Jefferson in the 1776 Declaration of Independence stated that the pursuit of happiness is a fundamental human right. That is a wonderful statement and gives us permission to find happiness in whatever way we can, providing we do not violate the happiness of others. But the difficulty for most people is how to achieve harmony and happiness in family, community, and national life. Creating a state that even remotely reflects the ideal life portrayed in the Rām Charit Mānasa is the last thing we think about in everyday life. Regrettably, surviving is sometimes the only strategy that makes sense.

Downward slide

It is difficult to talk about being happy without comparing it to times when we are less happy, or the worst times when we experience no happiness at all. After all, if it is a fundamental right to be happy, why, according to the 2022 World Happiness Report, has there been a gradual decline in enjoyment of life?

The facts are not encouraging. The latest Negative Experience Index indicates that unhappiness continued its dismal rise in 2021, "as the world overall became a sadder, more worried and more stressed-out place," while the Positive Experience Index dropped for the first time in years.[3] These outcomes are confirmed by the World Happiness Report, which states, "There has, on average, been a long-term moderate upward trend in stress, worry, and sadness in most countries and a slight long-term decline in the enjoyment of life."[4] As noted in the Introduction, COVID-19 cannot be entirely blamed for the decline in happiness levels as worry and stress have been quietly increasing over the last ten years.

There are many possible reasons for this change: our behavioral patterns, how we think and what we do; feeling stressed and wanting to isolate; alcohol and drug dependency; fatigue and feelings of failure; even lack of exercise, sleep, and proper nutrition. Contributing factors include political and economic anxieties; or thinking that life is meaningless and has no purpose. Most people feel unhappy at some time in their lives but too many people experience some or many of these segues into unhappiness too often with measurable effects on society. And just to add to this, a joint statement by the World Health Organization and the International Labor Organization pointed out that an estimated 12 billion workdays "are lost annually due to depression and anxiety costing the global economy nearly US $1 trillion."[5]

Global depression

According to the Mayo Clinic, depression "is a mood disorder that causes a persistent feeling of sadness and loss of interest."[6] Hence, depression is more than just temporary feelings of sadness but is a condition that affects everything we do, how we think, how we feel, and how we behave. Symptoms of depression are not always easy to define, but the worst are feelings of insignificance; of being worthless and not wanting to go on. Sadly, this latter can lead to suicide.

About 280 million people worldwide suffer from depressive episodes, which are considered a major contributor to levels of global disease. The World Health Organization identifies three types of depression:

- single episode depressive disorder, meaning the person's first and only episode
- recurrent depressive disorder, meaning the person has a history of at least two depressive episodes
- bipolar disorder, meaning that depressive episodes alternate with periods of manic symptoms, which include euphoria or irritability, increased activity or energy, and other symptoms such as increased talkativeness, racing thoughts, increased self-esteem, decreased need for sleep, distractibility, and impulsive reckless behavior.[7]

These figures do not make for comfortable reading. While the World Happiness Report indicates that overall happiness has risen slightly in the U.S., depression is still a problem. Approximately 8.4% of Americans (21 million at the last count) have suffered at least one major depressive episode in their lives, and young people are also affected.

The world's children

As mentioned by *The State of the World's Children*, 2021, "Roughly 1 in 5 young people aged 15–24 said they often feel depressed or have little interest in doing things."[8] This is a tragedy because young people are the nation's greatest gift to the future. How does it help the future if young people are damaged by conflict, and deprived of access to protection and support? How does it help when social media, according to *The Guardian* newspaper, has taken "a lot of character out of young people's communication and left a lot of them strangers to themselves."[9] Social media has its advantages, but it has disadvantages as well, which come in the form of loneliness due to the lack of face-to-face community contact, and anxiety due to the knowledge that everything is recorded online, seemingly forever. This latter issue is disastrous as it threatens the obvious fact that we can change our lives completely.

Disappointment is an added problem. The Japanese company Yakult reported that in the U.K., thanks to COVID restrictions, many young people are completely disillusioned:[10]

- 89% of 16–29-year-olds believe that their lives have no meaning or purpose
- 30% believe they are stuck in a rut
- 84% believe they are failing to "live their best life."

These figures did improve with age, except that about 55% of the over-60s gave similar answers.

Polls in other Western countries have shown similar results, and in Europe, there has been a worrying increase in suicides or suicidal thoughts among the young.[11] Something has gone wrong, and even if the COVID-19 pandemic is not the sole cause, it has not helped. Yet all is not doom and gloom.

Light out of darkness

There is a heartwarming aspect to the reports coming out. Figures from Yakult indicate that over half the British people (51%) believe we are on earth to be as happy as we can be, a little over a third believe that we should help others to be happy, and another third believe our purpose should be to do as much good as we can. These trends may well be reflected in other countries. The report certainly suggests there is no shortage of compassion. Indeed, one of the good things that the recent World Health Report has highlighted has been the huge rise in benevolence, or kindness, during 2021. This finding is supported by the 2022 World Happiness Report, which also notes a big increase in social care. The COVID pandemic had an unprecedented reach, and yet with all the tragedy and suffering, individuals from every part of the globe have been willing to offer much needed support and a greater willingness to reach out to others. In addition, more people than ever have donated to charity, jumped into voluntary work, and acted as good Samaritans to perfect strangers.[12]

Good Samaritans are heroes of any age. Think of the woman who collapsed on a Chicago street and the doctor who just happened to be passing by and rushed over to give her life-saving CPR.[13] Or the mysterious Dallas man who pulled to safety a woman trapped in a car about to be engulfed in flames.[14] And let's not forget the man who responded to a desperate Facebook message from a woman trying to make contact with her elderly mother as Hurricane Ian roared through the east coast. The man, again a stranger, waded through chest-high floodwater to find the mother and make sure she was safe.[15] None of these heroes had ever met the people they saved, but lives were at stake, and they stepped up to help.

Everyone can face periods when the lights are turned off and everything goes dark. In these times, we cannot just close our eyes, harden our hearts, and "get over it." Feelings are important and recovering from a tragedy takes time, work, and a huge amount of energy. In addition, in situations of anger, the hardest feeling of all is difficult to generate, and that is forgiveness. Forgiveness is based on an increase of compassion for someone else, and love. But having so much love that it is possible to forgive even our worst enemy, or our nation's, cannot be produced to order. A small cup can only contain a certain amount of water, and the cup needs to expand if more water, or love, is to be contained.

Families are the first place in which we seek and give love, gain a sense of community, and learn the importance of taking care of the needs of others as well as ourselves. The love that is generated in a family is the ground of our future relationships. Strong family love helps young people forge secure, strong attachments, and it is the same thing for the family of nations. When nations develop the habit of taking care of the needs of all countries and all people, then they will be creating the foundation for global happiness.

Chapter 2

The Puzzle of Happiness

In order to be happy oneself it is necessary to make at least one other person happy ... The secret of human happiness is not in self-seeking but in self-forgetting.

Theodor Reik[1]

When questioned, most people would probably describe being happy as a contented feeling, an uplifting sensation, something that brings satisfaction to their lives. The only problem here is that one individual's happiness may conflict with another person's happiness. A very simple example is when a neighbor acquires a puppy that likes to bark especially at night, and the next-door-neighbor wants a good night's sleep. But there are more serious cases. What happens when the leader of the Russian Federation hungers to end Ukrainian statehood and Ukraine is determined to retain its statehood? The result is conflict of the kind that brings unhappiness to both Russia and Ukraine, and to the wider world family. As we have seen, in addition to the tragedies of war, the outcome of this conflict has been gas and grain shortages and a threat to global economic growth, containing a raft of dangerous consequences.

Happiness is something we all want, something that we aspire to in our activities, and clearly, something we believe is a right. We can feel happy when we are in a close loving relationship, watching a high-profile wedding, or celebrating a big win, but these types of happiness may not last. We adapt quickly, the euphoria fades, and the old loneliness or insecurities creep back in.

According to research, whether or not we can reach a state of happiness depends on three factors: (a) our genetic makeup,

(b) our circumstances, and (c) our activities and practices.[2] We are not imprisoned by our genes, however, because gene expression can change. Genes can be turned on or off, or they can be made to work in a different way due to the food, drugs, or toxins we take in from the environment. "You are what you eat" is not just a common expression, it is a reality according to scientific research. The Centers for Disease Control study on epigenetics states:

> Your genes play an important role in your health, but so do your behaviors and environment, such as what you eat and how physically active you are. Epigenetics is the study of how your behaviors and environment can cause changes that affect the way your genes work. Unlike genetic changes, epigenetic changes are reversible and do not change your DNA sequence, but they can change how your body reads a DNA sequence.[3]

Thus, "we are what we eat" is an important factor for increasing well-being especially if we consider "what we eat" in terms of everything we digest, whether it is food and drink, or the movies and TV shows we watch. The very experiences we have change the brain, and the brain is responsible for, among other things, our ability to think and feel emotions, including the emotion of happiness.

In the past, neuroscientists thought that once the brain was fully assembled at about the age of 25, the brain could not change. But in one of the most revolutionary discoveries of the 20th century, scientists discovered that every experience we have "leaves a trace in the brain."[4]

This phenomenon is named *neural plasticity*, a term that suggests we can replace unwanted habits that create depression with habits that foster happiness by putting our attention on the activities and experiences we want to have. Moreover, research by Sonja Lyubomirsky and colleagues indicates that happiness-related activities are the best means we have for increasing happiness, as they can reduce unwanted effects from our genes.[5] Slightly pessimistically, the researchers refer to other studies suggesting that we adapt to changes so quickly that any happiness we initially experience dissipates once we get used to the change. But at the least, joyful activities are a good place to start.

A different happiness

Happiness means different things to different people. Ice skating, for instance, might be a source of happiness for some but a complete nightmare for others. Many people want happiness to be instantaneous, and there are ways of achieving this. For instance, 20 years of research from International Flavors & Fragrances, Inc. indicate that fragrances can influence mood and emotions.[6] Moreover, the IFF has developed a self-report method called Mood Mapping™ that reliably measures the mood associations of aromas, whether simple ingredients or finished fragrances in consumer products.[7] Mood Mapping offers a "choice of eight mood categories to panelists, who are asked to smell the aroma of a sample and 'pick the mood category that best matches the aroma of the sample.'"[8] An example is seen with the voting results for clementines versus vanilla: panelists found the aroma of clementines and the aroma of vanilla to be equally pleasant, but they favored clementines for stimulation and vanilla for relaxation.

Use and misuse of drugs

Nevertheless, people also seek happiness in more questionable ways. Recreational drugs are one of these, and the U.S. is experiencing an epidemic of drug overdoses, since that is probably the biggest risk today, at least for some drugs. But the type of happiness offered by recreational drugs (and alcohol must be included in this category) is neither reliable nor risk-free. Loss of control while under the influence of such drugs can lead to undesirable or even tragic outcomes; the cost of drugs can drive users to theft; the HIV virus can be transferred via needle sharing; and overdoses are, regrettably, not uncommon. Even legal drugs, if misused in pursuit of some short-lived burst of happiness, have unwanted side effects. Here are two examples:

- Anabolic steroids, referred to by their abusers as stackers, gear, or juice, build muscle mass, but overuse can lead to heart problems, high blood pressure, or kidney and liver damage. These drugs can also cause extreme anger, aggression, or delusions.
- Benzodiazepines, used to treat insomnia, anxiety, and panic attack disorders, are calming as they slow down blood pressure, breathing, and heart rates. They are also highly addictive. If they are abused, which does happen, then the abuser risks abnormally slow breathing (bradypnea) and overdose.

Vine of the soul

Ayahuasca, which means "vine of the ancestors" or "vine of the soul" in the indigenous Quechua language recognized in Ecuador, Peru, and Bolivia, is a psychoactive drug made from the *Banisteriopsis caapi* plant, native to regions of the Amazon. Ayahuasca is drunk as a tea, but the tea can contain other ingredients, including *Erythroxylum coca,* cocaine, Nicotiana (including nicotine), *Brugmansia* (containing scopolamine), and Ilex guayusa, which has caffeine.

It gets more complicated as the added ingredients also include *Psychotria viridis*, known as the chacruna plant, which in its turn contains DMT, a Schedule 1 psychedelic substance that is illegal in the U.S. DMT (N, N-dimethyltryptamine) is a tryptamine, meaning that it is a metabolite of tryptophan, an amino acid. Sometimes known as Dimitri, DMT is the psychedelic substance that is responsible for the extreme hallucinations, visions, or altered states of consciousness that some people experience with ayahuasca. DMT also appears to decrease the blood flow to the brain,[9] and this can be dangerous because decreased blood flow has the potential to damage brain cells and result in negative health issues such as dizziness, nausea, and shortness of breath.

It is a complex area. The complete mixture of ayahuasca, containing MAOIs (harmala alkaloids) has been used to treat depression. However, it is impossible to say from studies "that DMT itself or the elevation of other brain neurotransmitters in combination is responsible for the perceived positive clinical effects or even if the hallucinations produced by DMT consumed under these conditions are themselves somehow cathartic."[10] The thing is, if DMT is ingested on its own, it will not affect the mind. Adding it to the ayahuasca vine, however, allows it to cross the blood-brain barrier, which can cause hallucinations lasting up to four hours. The question is, does drinking ayahuasca bring lasting happiness? It may for some people, but as the drug becomes more known, so do the potential side effects—vomiting, diarrhea, paranoia, and panic, and more seriously according to WebMD, seizures, respiratory arrest, and coma.[11] Finally, the conclusion to a 2018 paper published in *Mental Health Clinician* suggests that "a publication bias toward favorable results may be present in the current literature."[12]

Transcendental experiences versus psychedelic drugs

There have been attempts to equate the effects of psychedelic drugs and meditation. This is an incorrect equation according to a new paper published in the *International Journal of Psychological Studies*.[13] The paper's author, Frederick Travis, Director of the Center for Brain, Consciousness, and Cognition at Maharishi International University, does encourage more research on the effects of both psychedelic drugs and transcendental experiences, but also emphasizes strong differences between them. For instance: while psychedelics are associated with decreased blood flow to the brain, transcendental experiences are characterized by higher blood flow in frontal areas of the brain. Moreover, psychedelic experiences are characterized by the functioning of localized circuits and gamma EEG, while transcendental experiences are characterized by the functioning of global circuits and alpha EEG.

In addition, the content of experiences differs between psychedelic drugs and transcendental experiences as do the mechanisms of effects. Evidence suggests that psychedelic drugs can be influenced by the set and setting while transcendental experiences transcend the set and setting. This is an important point as Dr. Travis explains.

> Casual use of psychedelics in uncontrolled settings could lead to extreme fear, anxiety, and mental instability. Even micro-dosing is reported to result in positive experiences half the time and negative experiences the other half. In addition, psychedelic-assisted therapy involves a single psychedelic experience rather than multiple psychedelic sessions over months or years.[14]

Finally, Travis questions the wisdom of micro-dosing (ingesting small amounts of ayahuasca and another psychedelic called psilocybin) to combat anxiety and depression. There are times when psychedelic drug intervention may be needed, but, according to Fred Travis, the problem seems to be that "the natural behaviors that would naturally result in elevated serotonin are not there to maintain stable levels."[15]

To put it another way, offering psychedelic drug intervention could be likened to building a house without a foundation, the foundation being the steady buildup of sustained levels of serotonin through more natural means. These might include exercise, a tryptophan-rich diet, and transcendental experiences, that allow well-being to become a stable reality.

It seems common sense to take a long-term view of achieving the kind of happiness and well-being that might be sustainable. Psychedelic drugs that can, in some cases, give a twisted view of reality to the user are unlikely to create sustained happiness either for the user, their families, or society. It may be that, like other drugs and cigarette smoking, a full understanding of the risks and side effects will only come with time.

Chapter 3

Power: Another Drug, or a Means to Happiness?

The rich philistinism emanating from advertisements is due not to their exaggerating (or inventing) the glory of this or that serviceable article but to suggesting that the acme of human happiness is purchasable and that its purchase somehow ennobles the purchaser.

Vladimir Nabukov[1]

According to research by Yona Kifer of Tel Aviv University and her colleagues, powerful people can "navigate their lives in congruence with their internal desires and inclinations."[2] The reason for this is that power increases the connections between the way we feel and the way we behave. Therefore, the authors of the research hypothesize that power enhances our subjective well-being by letting us feel more "authentic." *Authentic* is a much-used word today. Basically, it means being true to ourselves, honest with ourselves and with others, and avoiding pretense. A caveat here is that "authentic" should not mean hurting others with our honesty. There is such a thing as speaking the sweet truth that is honest yet kind and uplifting. If we are being true to ourselves, then, apparently, we are more content with our lives. The only caveat here is that our personalities, beliefs, and feelings are not set in stone; they change as we mature and as we reject some things and accept others. Being true to ourselves makes more sense if we not only recognize and accept the fact that we change but look more deeply into the essence of ourselves—who we really are. This is true authenticity and is covered later in the book.

Yona Kifer's team carried out three experiments. In the first, 350 participants were surveyed to see if inner feelings of power were tied to subjective well-being in the contexts of work, romantic relationships, and friends. In a fascinating study, the outcomes demonstrated that the most powerful people in any of these contexts tended to be more content.

- 16% experienced greater satisfaction with their lives compared to the least powerful people as seen primarily at work; and
- powerful employees experienced a 26% increase in job satisfaction compared to colleagues who were considered powerless.

However, in the categories of romantic relationships and friends, the results indicated a smaller percentage.

- In only 18% of romantic relationships were powerful romantic partners more satisfied.
- With friendships, this figure shrank to 11%.

The researchers consider that in terms of friendships, such a low figure might be due to the fact that friendships are associated with feelings of community rather than power rankings.

In the second and third experiments, Yona Kifer and colleagues evaluated the causal relationship between power, feelings of authenticity, and general well-being by manipulating each of these independently. The results showed that power causes people to feel more "true to themselves" in the sense that there is a close bond between beliefs, desires, and actions. Hence, in the minds of the researchers, feelings of authenticity increase subjective feelings of well-being and happiness.

Authenticity

While the importance of authenticity is supported by earlier research, which suggests that authenticity is integral to well-being,[3] more recent research exploring the relationship between authenticity, well-being, and employee engagement suggests that the bond between authenticity and well-being is stronger in the West than it is in the East. The reason for this may be due to the "collectivist" nature of Eastern cultures. Collectivist cultures exist where a group emphasizes the needs of the collective over the needs of an individual within the group. Anna Sutton from the University of Waikato in New Zealand states, "In general, the more collectivist a culture is, the weaker the positive relationship between authenticity and well-being."[4] This finding confirms the suggestion that in collectivist cultures, a tendency to be true to oneself may come into conflict with the interests of the group as a whole.

On a final note, Yona Kifer and her colleagues point out, "Although striving for power lowers well-being, these results demonstrate the pervasive positive psychological effects of having power, and indicate the importance of spreading power to enhance collective well-being."[5]

But however true this conclusion may be, adding and spreading happiness by achieving power can be fraught with danger, since power has a tendency to breed the desire for more power. In the worst-case scenarios, Hitler's greed for power resulted in a horrific world war. Stalin caused the deaths of millions through famine and terror concentration camps. Mao was responsible for the deaths of approximately 1.5 million people in the cultural revolution and anywhere up to 45 million during the great famine. And Cambodia's Pol Pot forced mass evacuations of cities, killed and displaced millions of his own people, and left his country impoverished. Clearly, achieving happiness through power needs to be handled with caution. It has the added challenge of being largely temporary as any historian knows.

Chapter 4

Eudaimonia: Living a Worthwhile Life

No man can live a happy life, or even a supportable life, without the study of wisdom.

Seneca the Younger[1]

Unsurprisingly, pursuing material wealth does not appear to bring long-lasting happiness, as confirmed by Robert Waldinger, a psychiatrist and the fourth director of the Harvard Study of Adult Development, one of the most complete studies of happiness ever carried out. For over 75 years, the Harvard study tracked the home lives, health, and work life of 724 men, without having any idea how the story of each life would play out. They examined the men's medical records, drew their blood, scanned their brains, and talked to their children. Out of the original 724 men, 60 were still alive and participating in the study in 2016. And now, the study is starting to look at the lives of the more than 2,000 children of these pioneering individuals.

Robert Waldinger spoke about the results of the Harvard study in a TED talk given in November 2015.[2] He noted that many young men begin adult life thinking that wealth and fame create the "good life," but the happiness of achieving fame and fortune can vanish completely if fame and fortune are diminished or altogether removed. A recent survey asked millennials to reveal their most important goals in life. A staggering 80% commented that their major goal was to be rich while 50% of the same millennials commented that their second major goal was to be famous. Yet in the end, according to the Harvard study, this is not enough.

Eudaimonic behavior

The discovery that wealth and fame do not necessarily create a good life is confirmed by a different body of research, published fourteen years ago, suggesting that "doing good" or helping others contributes to a far more meaningful and happier life than pursuing material gain.[3] In this study, lead researcher Michael Steger suggested that greater well-being comes with engaging in "eudaimonic" behaviors, "inherently meaningful endeavors" resulting in an increased sense of well-being the following day. "Eudaimonic" is a Greek word referring to a life well lived, or to a deeper happiness that transcends the hedonistic opposites, pursuing pleasure and avoiding pain. Eudaimonic happiness is the opposite to hedonic happiness, a term that can be traced back to the Greek philosopher Aristippus and the Cyrenaic school of philosophy. It all comes down to the end goal of life, or what we think is the end goal of life. For Aristippus, the end goal was pleasure, fine food, and wine. Luckily, he also thought that his followers should apply good judgment and use self-control to moderate strong human desires; otherwise, the result might have been chaos and misery for others.

Michael Steger and his colleagues conducted two studies, both of which showed that eudaimonic behaviors were more closely associated with well-being than activities aimed at obtaining pleasure. The conclusion was that doing good for others might be a significant avenue through which people could create "meaningful and satisfying lives" for themselves.[4] Perhaps that is why there is such a heartwarming aspect to the Yakult report (see Chapter 1), which suggests that many young people think their purpose is to do as much good for others as they can. Such thinking is eudaimonic and would have pleased the Greek philosopher Aristotle. He also believed that happiness was final, self-sufficient, the end of action,[5] and "a virtuous activity of soul," or to put it another way, the result of honorable living.[6]

In tandem with Aristotle, the philosopher Plato also held that happiness is not some temporary pleasure or satisfaction but is found in a life of virtue and goodness.[7] Plato expected citizens to do their duty, and maintained that if they did, then their happiness would be assured.[8] In regard to government, Plato was well aware of lesser states of happiness when he spoke of the happiness of the "tyrant."

In the early days of his tyranny he smiles and beams upon everybody; he is not a 'dominus,' no, not he: he has only come to put an end to debt and the monopoly of land. Having got rid of foreign enemies, he makes himself necessary to the State by always going to war. He is thus enabled to depress the poor by heavy taxes, and so keep them at work; and he can get rid of bolder spirits by handing them over to the enemy. Then comes unpopularity; some of his old associates have the courage to oppose him. The consequence is, that he has to make a purgation of the State; but, unlike the physician who purges away the bad, he must get rid of the high-spirited, the wise and the wealthy; for he has no choice between death and a life of shame and dishonour. And the more hated he is, the more he will require trusty guards; but how will he obtain them? 'They will come flocking like birds—for pay.' Will he not rather obtain them on the spot? He will take the slaves from their owners and make them his body-guard; these are his trusted friends, who admire and look up to him. Are not the tragic poets wise who magnify and exalt the tyrant, and say that he is wise by association with the wise? And are not their praises of tyranny alone a sufficient reason why we should exclude them from our State?[9]

Plato reserved some of his strongest condemnation for tyrannical leaders, believing them to descend into helpless misery; the opposite to happiness. Hence, on the individual level, happiness between one person and another comes from giving and receiving the emotion of love; on the national level, happiness in government comes from fulfilling the needs of the people and enjoying the love and respect that comes back from them; and on the international level, happiness between nations occurs when every nation is fulfilled and looks to nurture and preserve fulfillment in every other nation.

The purpose of life

When two parties, whether national or personal, each act in such a way as to bring satisfaction to the other, then happiness has a better chance of flowing like a stream down a mountain. As the founder of the Transcendental Meditation organization, Maharishi Mahesh Yogi, states,

> Happiness has certainly to be taken into account while considering the performance of any action, because the aim of any action is the increase of happiness — the very purpose of creation and of evolution is expansion of happiness. So, if happiness does not result from an action, then that action defeats the very purpose of action, and its performance cannot be justified.[10]

Happiness has many levels, from supreme happiness of a permanent nature, through the happiness resulting from living a life that brings maximum satisfaction to ourselves and contributes to the welfare of others, to the transient moments of happiness that are the day-to-day experience of most people. Nonetheless, it is perfectly possible that people who are very happy can enjoy both eudaimonic and hedonic aspects of happiness. In other words, they live their lives well, contribute to the well-being of others, and at the same time enjoy material gain. But power in itself cannot be the ultimate key to happiness because powerful people can still have unhappy marriages, need therapy, feel lonely, and worse, struggle to maintain power, experience stress, and face their fair share of disappointment.

Plato and Aristotle were aligned with the idea that eudaimonic behaviors increase a sense of personal well-being, as does Michael Steger in our own time. But, perhaps one of the most famous contemporary psychologists, whose hierarchy of needs champions the eudaimonic perspective, was the influential American psychologist Abraham Maslow.

Abraham Maslow

As you see in the table below, Abraham Maslow envisioned a hierarchy of five needs that still stand as a model of human happiness.

5	Self-actualization	Achieving our full potential—Health, Happiness, Fulfillment
4	Esteem	Prestige and feelings of accomplishment
3	Belongingness and love	Intimate relationships and friends
2	Safety	Security and safety
1	Physiological	Food, water, warmth, rest (continues throughout all levels)

Abraham Maslow's Hierarchy of Needs

Each level of need refers to a level of happiness. The first is the basic biological need for food, water, warmth, and rest. These are needs that are essential for human survival and continue throughout all other states. The second level refers to security. This not only includes physical safety; it embraces economic and social safety, neither of which are easy to find in times of conflict. Then comes the need for a sense of accomplishment, something that increases our self-esteem and self-confidence. The fourth level emphasizes our need to belong, to feel that we are loved and have friends and intimate relationships that sustain us through challenging times. The final stage is self-actualization where we become the best person we can be by fulfilling our potential. This is the highest happiness for Maslow, the level of peak experiences, which, while temporary, are still moments where we can experience transcendence of self.

Maslow describes self-actualized people in this way:

Self-actualizing people, those who have come to a high level of maturation, health, and self-fulfillment, have so much to teach us that sometimes they seem almost like a different breed of human beings. But, because it is so new, the exploration of the highest reaches of human nature and of its ultimate possibilities and aspirations is a difficult and tortuous task. It has involved for me the continuous destruction of cherished axioms, the perpetual coping with seeming paradoxes, contradictions and vagueness and the occasional collapse around my ears of long established, firmly believed in and seemingly unassailable laws of psychology.[11]

The list of signs that confirm a self-actualized state include a "zest in living, of happiness or euphoria, of serenity, of joy, of calmness, of responsibility, of confidence in one's ability to handle stresses, anxieties, and problems."[12] In line with this, Maslow states his belief in a single, ultimate value.

It looks as if there were a single ultimate value for mankind, a far goal toward which all men strive. This is called variously by different authors self-actualization, self-realization, integration, psychological health, individuation, autonomy, creativity, productivity, but they all agree that this amounts to realizing the potentialities of the person, that is to say, becoming fully human, everything that the person can become.[13]

As described by Maslow, these "peak experiences" are moments of pure joy that eclipse every other joyful moment. Their memory can last, bring great comfort, and be likened to a spiritual experience. Spirituality can always be described in different ways, but basically, it is a universal human experience, described in a paper by Acceptance and Commitment Therapist (ACT) Eltica de Jager Meezenbroek and her colleagues as the "experience of connection with oneself, connectedness with others and nature, and connectedness with the transcendent."[14]

Maslow's hierarchy of needs has influenced other psychologists such as Carol Ryff who called on his thinking to form her own theory of well-being through eudaimonic behavior. For Carol Ryff, more research is needed to address "problems of unjust societies wherein greed among privileged elites may be a force compromising the eudaimonic well-being of those less privileged." She also discusses "the need to better understand the role of the arts, broadly defined, in promoting eudaimonic well-being across all segments of society."[15]

Happiness, or well-being, may be an elusive emotion to define in words, but nowadays, individual happiness levels can be measured through research on different moods, different lifestyles, and changes in biochemistry. Even the overall happiness and well-being of society can be measured through wide-scale surveys such as the World Happiness Report, or the World Health Report. Even so, however useful it is to *gauge* the mood and well-being of society, it is equally important to *improve* the well-being and quality of life throughout society.

As described in the next chapter, and confirmed by extensive research, one novel means to improve the well-being and happiness of society is through Transcendental Meditation practice. More than 400 published, peer-reviewed studies have shown that TM practice can reduce stress and promote inner peace and happiness for the individuals who make up society. But what exactly is Transcendental Meditation?

Chapter 5

The Transcendental Meditation Technique

Extensive research, including randomized controlled trials, has documented the benefits of the Transcendental Meditation technique for reducing symptoms of PTS and suicidal ideation, as well as decreasing stress, anxiety, depression, substance use disorder, and heart disease; improving brain and cognitive functioning; and raising performance.

General James "Spider" Marks[1]

There are many meditation techniques that are effective in one way or another, or to some degree or another. These range from breathing techniques to practices associated with religions. There is even a chocolate meditation.[2] The idea behind this seems to be to transcend through the sense of taste. As yet, there is little published research in peer-reviewed journals on this form of meditation. But if transcending through the sense of taste is a genuine method of increasing happiness, studies may come in the future.

Whichever meditation we choose is based on how we feel and what we resonate with. Our personal path to happiness is our own and not necessarily the same as anyone else's path. I am delighted for each reader to find their own unique path, but there is not the time nor space in this book to go through every single technique. Hence, I have stuck with the technique I am most familiar with as I practice it myself: the Transcendental Meditation technique.

The Transcendental Meditation technique
The practice of Transcendental Meditation was brought to the West in 1959 by Maharishi Mahesh Yogi, a leading Vedic

scholar and scientist of consciousness. He revived numerous programs from the ancient Vedic tradition of knowledge preserved in India to bring people back in touch with their deepest self. Additionally, Maharishi, as he is known in the world, introduced meditation to the world of modern scientific research and thus opened a connection between objective measurement and the subjective world of the Self, which, as we will see, is Transcendental Consciousness, an underlying field of consciousness with effects that can be measured.

Transcendental Meditation has been taught to over ten million people from all population groups. It is a simple, natural, effortless technique that is practiced for 20 minutes morning and evening without requiring any change in beliefs or lifestyle. The technique of Transcendental Meditation is effective, reliable, and safe. Literally hundreds of studies, conducted at more than 200 independent universities and research institutions and published in peer-reviewed medical and scientific journals, have shown evidence that it can reduce stress, depression, and anxiety, and increase well-being and happiness. Transcendental Meditation, however, is not just about reducing blood pressure or stress. Experiences which take place during a typical Transcendental Meditation session can answer many of the big questions that most people have, and since the experiences can bring personal comfort and greater connection with the world around us, they can increase levels of inner peace and happiness.

Endorsing happiness

Anecdotal reports of happiness through Transcendental Meditation are plentiful. For instance, below is a report from David Lynch, moviemaker, and founder of the David Lynch Foundation (DLF). The aim of the DLF is to "prevent and eradicate the all-pervasive epidemic of trauma and toxic stress among at-risk populations through promoting widespread implementation of the evidence-based Transcendental Meditation (TM) program in order to improve their health, cognitive capabilities and performance in life."[3] David Lynch has experienced these benefits firsthand.

> When I had my first meditation, this inner bliss revealed itself so powerfully—thick happiness came rushing in. And I said, "This is it." There it was. And everything just started getting better—way more fun, way more joy in the doing. Everything just got better and better. I didn't think about not getting angry—the anger just lifted away. And what they say is when you start infusing this transcendence, you don't really realize that anger is going. It's other people close to you that see it first. And it just seems natural. You're happy, and there's nothing you can do about it. You just get happier.[4]

Commenting on an experience of feeling that everything was right, in the right place, at the right time, a feeling of total security and evenness, no matter what, another TM practitioner stated:

> For me, this quality has been growing with TM practice. The happiness I feel deep inside with my eyes closed in meditation spills over into activity. Silence forms the platform upon which action occurs. I am completely engaged and involved in a creative task. When it finishes, I move seamlessly to the next. The activity brings out more of those qualities of appropriateness and fidelity that I now associate with loving attention to detail. I call this being happily in the flow.
> D.F.[5]

Three categories of meditation

The effects of different techniques of meditation on the human physiology will vary, and these variations can be evaluated and compared. For instance, an effect found in one type of meditation, such as Transcendental Meditation, cannot necessarily be applied to another type of meditation.[6] The reason is that the multitude of meditation approaches fall into three distinct categories: focused attention meditation, which involves voluntary and sustained attention on a chosen object; open monitoring, or mindfulness-based meditations, which involve nonreactive monitoring of the moment-to-moment content of experience;[7] and automatic self-transcending, where the procedures of the technique are transcended; practitioners go beyond the surface level of our awareness and experience deep inner silence.

Figure 1. Three categories of meditation. (Cited in *An Antidote to Violence: Evaluating the Evidence* by Barry Spivack & Patricia Saunders.)

Different EEG Signature

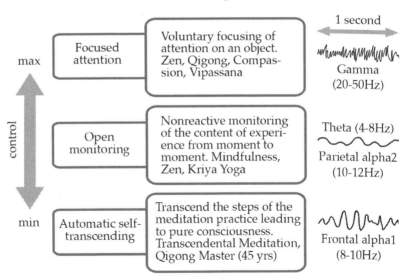

The three main categories of meditation, Focused Attention, Open Monitoring, and Automatic Self-transcending are characterized by unique brain signatures. This provides a neuro-physiological method of distinguishing between the three.

As shown in the above chart, focused attention is primarily concentration and is a process whereby practitioners control the contents of meditation. With this type of technique, the mind continually focuses on a particular object, and if the mind wanders off, it is brought back to the object of attention. Focused attention techniques, generally, demonstrate electroencephalographic (EEG) signatures characterized by EEG frequencies in the beta-2 (20–30 Hz) and gamma (30–50 Hz) frequency bands. Techniques in this category include loving-kindness-compassion, Qigong, and Diamond Way Buddhism.[8]

Open monitoring techniques display EEG frequencies in the theta range (5–8 Hz) and involve the non-judgmental monitoring of ongoing experience. With these types of meditations, individual attention is open and observes whatever is happening, whether it be the breath, the thoughts, or bodily sensations. Open monitoring techniques are based on an awareness of sensory, cognitive, and affective fields of experience in the present moment and involve a higher-order meta-awareness of ongoing mental processes. Meditations in this category include Vipassana, Zazen, Sahaja Yoga, and Concentrative Qigong, an ancient method of synchronized physical postures, breathing, and meditation related to Tai Chi.[9]

Automatic self-transcending

Since Transcendental Meditation fits into neither the focused attention nor the open monitoring categories, Dr. Frederick Travis (director of the Center for the Brain, Consciousness, and Cognition), and Dr. Jonathan Shear from the Department of Philosophy, Virginia Commonwealth University, suggested a third category of meditation, automatic self-transcending.[10] Automatic self-transcending is characterized by alpha-1 (8–10 Hz) activity and is experienced as an effortless method of transcending the steps of the meditation. Put simply, automatic self-transcending effortlessly allows the attention of the mind to turn inward, settle down, and experience the source of thought.

Figure 2. From the surface to the transcendent. (Cited in *An Antidote to Violence*: *Evaluating the Evidence* by Barry Spivack & Patricia Saunders.)

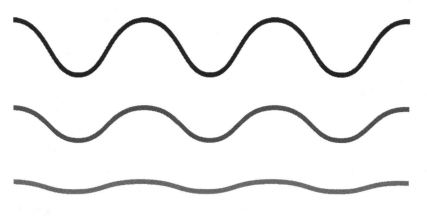

The waves at the surface of this illustration represent the more excited levels of the mind experienced with waking state consciousness. During Transcendental Meditation practice, however, the mind, whilst remaining alert, becomes less excited, and this is represented by the shallower waves. As the less excited states of the mind are increasingly more charming, the mind naturally and spontaneously settles down to a state of least excitation, or Transcendental Consciousness, represented by the straight line. On the level of human physiology, this is known as a state of restful alertness.

The key word is "effortlessly." The effortlessness of any meditation practice can be verified by the level of activity in the default mode network (DMN), a brain network encompassing areas in the front and the back of the brain that is active when we are not focused on the outside world. According to research by Dr. Travis, the DMN goes down when we focus, and increases during internal processing, or self-referential activity (the processing of information relevant to oneself).[11] With the Transcendental Meditation technique, the DMN is high, indicating that the transcending process is effortless and not directed by cognitive control, but by an automatic procedure that does not involve control.[12] In addition, peer-reviewed research indicates that automatic self-transcending, unlike the other categories, also has a quantifiable effect on collective consciousness. (Collective consciousness is explained in Chapter 17.)

Not just stress release

Transcendental Meditation has two levels to it. At the deepest level, it gives answers to the big questions in life, the questions that cross everyone's mind at some point. The answers to these questions and others are bound up in our ability to think, to feel, and to organize ourselves. In other words, they are bound up in our consciousness and our understanding of consciousness—what it is, how far does it reach, and whether it can transform itself or us. Thus, Transcendental Meditation practice can increase the feeling that life has meaning if that feeling is already there, or generate a sense of meaning if it does not yet exist. And if we feel that life has meaning, then we are more likely to experience a greater sense of fulfillment and happiness. Happiness can be volatile, of course; one moment up, and the next minute down. That is why we naturally long for an inner happiness that is not dependent on outside circumstances. This does not mean we should not enjoy outside events; it just means we need to develop inner happiness to offset the times when the outside world does not bring as much joy.

Here are the experiences of two individuals who, like so many, thought that happiness could only come from others ... until they found the opposite.

When I was a young undergraduate student, I thought that my happiness was dependent on outer circumstances. I often enjoyed the company of a close friend for activities such as dining, walking, and attending plays.

One evening, in the early spring, I happened to be walking alone in a lovely garden. I quite remember seeing a magnolia tree with fresh, tender blossoms and the moon was gently rising. As I walked along, I experienced great joy flowing with every object that I perceived. Toward the end of my walk, I realized that the happiness and fulfillment that I experience in any situation, comes from deep within myself. S.K.[13]

And this from a student:

Sometimes, in a quiet moment, a feeling comes over me and I remember that this is how happiness feels. At other times, I'll be busily doing something and have the realization that a baseline of happiness, which is not contingent on anything outside of me, is present. But before learning TM, I never thought that happiness could be a daily phenomenon, yet alone the birthright of me and everyone else. Live and learn. M.Y.[14]

These individuals were fortunate to find a very real happiness in such a pleasant way. Others find a similar happiness but in a hard way. For instance, incarceration in the harsh conditions of prison in the 1970s must have been one of the most miserable experiences that anyone could have. For Pat Corum, misery was an everyday reality of life, at least to begin with.

Freedom in prison

Pat Corum spent 25 years in prison for two homicides. He was mostly in Folsom Prison, California's maximum-security facility and the subject of Johnny Cash's famous song *Folsom Prison Blues*. The final line of the song is "I'd let that lonesome whistle blow my blues away." Well, for Pat Corum, it was not a whistle that blew his blues away, but the Transcendental Meditation technique. Pat is quoted as saying that before he learned Transcendental Meditation, the only time he felt powerful was when he had a gun in his hand. After he learned Transcendental Meditation, he began to see life differently.

> In October 1975, I wrote a letter to Governor Brown stating that after 13 years in prison, I could honestly say that the TM program is the only program that has ever helped me. There are no ignorant changes or psychiatrist playing mind games. Everything has been positive from the moment I learned the TM technique. Besides being relaxed, feeling good, and being less rigid, I experienced a continual growth of inner strength, self-confidence, and self-esteem.[15]

Pat Corum chose to seek inner happiness, and through his TM practice, the stress of the past subsided. It was one of those strange times when a dark place offered the opportunity for a better life. Later, when speaking to Maharishi Mahesh Yogi, he thanked him on behalf of the "thousands of men and women incarcerated in the California Department of Corrections" for the opportunity to learn meditation.[16] Today, attitudes have changed and there are more criminal rehabilitation methods in use in prison systems in many countries. Norway probably leads the way, as its prison system focuses on humanizing inmates and encouraging normal everyday life activities such as exercise and socialization. In fact, apart from the lack of freedom, all other aspects of Norwegian prison life aim to reduce stress and generate feelings of calm and restoration; basically helping inmates to better themselves. And after five years of introducing these kinds of rehabilitation programs, Norway's recidivism rates have dropped significantly.[17] So, what would happen if Transcendental Meditation practice was added to the mix?

Generally speaking, one of the greatest problems of prison life, as in non-prison life, is the problem of stress and how to deal with it. Thus, the next chapter discusses diverse forms of stress and how the Transcendental Meditation technique can help decrease the trauma of stress.

Chapter 6

Reducing Stress

"You say the ring is dangerous, far more dangerous than I guess. In what way?"

"In many ways," answered the wizard. "It is far more powerful than I ever dared to think at first, so powerful that in the end it would utterly overcome anyone of mortal race who possessed it. It would possess him."

J.R.R. Tolkien[1]

If we swap the word "ring" with the word "stress," then the dangerous nature of excess stress becomes clear. Stress, like the fictional ring of power, can make people act in ways they would not normally do. Even the idea that "stress is good for you" is somewhat questionable. As Alfie Kohn, a writer on behavior and education, comments:

> To talk about input and output, stimulus and response, is to ignore the human being who stands in between, who constructs meaning around what he or she encounters, who arrives on the scene with expectations, goals, fears, a distinctive point of view. Thus, pressure might spur people to jump higher or memorize more facts. But is the point to avoid failure or to achieve success? Those are two very different things. Failure-avoidance is what we'd expect in response to pressure, such as during a competition—that's much less likely to prove constructive over time, particularly if open-ended thinking is required.[2]

Some people do well under pressure, but others do not. In either case, the goal should be to become a successful human

41

being living a happy and fulfilled life rather than succumbing to the dangerous pressures of outside expectations. Becoming a successful human being occurs faster with experiences of Transcendental Consciousness, the state of inner silence that, as explained in the introduction to the book, is held to be the Self, the One, the Tao, or Samādhi in the Yoga tradition. Transcendental Consciousness is experienced when the mind settles down through finer and finer levels of thought until it goes beyond all thoughts and feelings and experiences a level of wakefulness with no content, no awareness of time or space, and where all memory of the conflicts of the relative world has vanished. It is consciousness awake to itself alone, and its essential nature is absolute bliss consciousness, or *Satchitānanda*: *Sat*, a Sanskrit word which can be translated as the ultimate and eternal truth of reality; *Chit*, meaning consciousness; and *Ānanda*, meaning bliss.[3]

The bliss and peace of transcendental experiences gives such warmth to the heart and deep rest to the mind that, given the connectivity between mind and body, deep-rooted stresses are dissolved effortlessly from the body, and we become the person we were always meant to be. The experience of Transcendental Consciousness (the Self) is also responsible for the release of stresses that may have been buried in the physiology for years. Stresses are the boundaries that prevent us from living our full potential, and collective stress is the boundary that prevents nations from expressing love and appreciation toward other nations. Once the stresses dissolve, then deeper levels of reality are more widely experienced and happiness in society and individual life is felt more fully.

Referring to Transcendental Consciousness and deep-rooted stress in the same breath is rather like being at the top of a great mountain where the sky is unbounded, and the air is fresh, and looking down to earth where the sky is hidden by clouds and the air is polluted. Yet, if we are to understand the full range of life, come down to earth we must.

Stress

Generally, when we think about stress, we think of problems and annoyance. Experiences of Transcendental Consciousness increase our happiness, but stress takes it away. The early 20th century Austrian-Canadian endocrinologist, Hans Selye, was the first person to use the word *stress* regarding the human experience. According to the American Institute of Stress, he stated that stress was "the non-specific response of the body to any demand for change." Over time, stress became a buzzword that is now understood as an overload on the mind or body. In this sense, there are three main types of stress:

- Long-term stress, experienced with long-term situations that cause anxiety, e.g., work that is not enjoyable, debilitating illness, difficult relationships
- Acute stress, experienced with sudden dangers, e.g., reacting to aggressive behavior or swerving in a car accident
- Traumatic stress experienced when faced with a life-threatening event, e.g., war, violence, or a riot.

All three categories are connected to the steroid hormone cortisol, frequently referred to as the "stress hormone," as it regulates our response to stress and affects almost every organ in our bodies. To be specific, cortisol activates the release of glucose (sugar) from the liver to give fast energy during moments of stress and increases the availability of substances that repair tissues. It also restrains functions that might be unnecessary in a stressful situation, for instance, digestion, the process of growth, and reproductive activity, and communicates with the regions of the brain that control fear or mood. Thus, although it is called the stress hormone, there is a great deal more to it than that.

Normal and acute stress

Normal stressful situations, such as suddenly braking to avoid a dog running across the road, do not last long. The threat is seen, action is taken, cortisol levels, which have increased, settle down, and the body returns to normal. Problems arise when cortisol is high over a long period of time, as in long-term stress. If cortisol stays high, it can disrupt the rest of the body's functions and increase the risk of anxiety, headaches, poor memory, depression, sleep problems, or heart disease. So, what does this have to do with Transcendental Meditation practice?

A random assignment study carried out in 1997 looked at two groups: one consisting of Transcendental Meditation practitioners, and the other, a control group using a stress education control protocol. The results indicated that with the TM group basal cortisol level and average cortisol during the study decreased from pre- to post-test as compared with controls. The conclusion was that the Transcendental Meditation technique reverses the effects of chronic stress significant for health.[4]

Stress and the heart

For those interested in heart disease, studies provide evidence that anxiety and hypertension, smoking, and alcohol abuse are significant risk factors for coronary heart disease as is stress. Exercise is known to help reduce stress, and so is spending time in a park setting. Researchers from the University of Alabama reported that spending as little as 20 minutes in a local urban park can improve emotional well-being, regardless of whether one is exercising or not.[5] Owning and caring for a pet can also reduce the risks of heart disease and lower unhealthy cholesterol levels, as does being out in nature, according to the American

Heart Association.[6] Finally, getting enough rest and practicing the Transcendental Meditation technique can substantially reduce stress.

Figure 3. Transcendental Meditation and the heart. (Cited in *An Antidote to Violence: Evaluating the Evidence* by Barry Spivack & Patricia Saunders.)

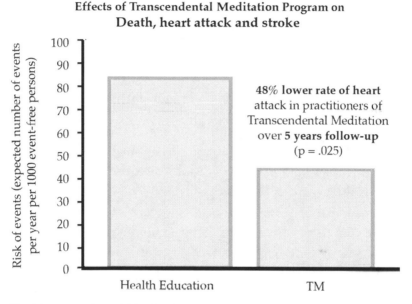

**Effects of Transcendental Meditation Program on
Death, heart attack and stroke**

48% **lower rate of heart** attack in practitioners of Transcendental Meditation over **5 years follow-up** (p = .025)

The Transcendental Meditation program significantly reduces risk factors for mortality, myocardial infarction and stroke in coronary heart disease patients. These changes are associated with lower blood pressure and psychosocial stress factors.

In a 2006 press release from the American Medical Association, the authors of a research study on Transcendental Meditation and cardiac risk factors stated: "These current results also expand our causal understanding of the role of stress in the rising epidemic of the metabolic syndrome. Although current low levels of physical activity, unhealthy eating habits and resultant obesity are triggers for this epidemic, the demands of modern society may also be responsible for higher levels of chronic stress." Such stress causes the release of cortisol and other hormones and neurotransmitters, which over time damage the cardiovascular system.

> Our results, demonstrating beneficial physiological effects of Transcendental Meditation in the absence of effects on psychosocial variables, suggest that Transcendental Meditation may modulate response to stress rather than alter the stress itself, similar to the physiological impact of exercise conditioning.[7]

Other studies followed, and then, in 2019, new and exciting research was published in the *Journal of Nuclear Cardiology*. The study, funded by the NIH (National Institutes of Health), assessed the combination of Transcendental Meditation with lifestyle changes. It involved 56 African-American patients suffering from different forms of heart disease who were assigned to one of four groups: Transcendental Meditation alone; a rehabilitation group consisting of diet and exercise changes; a TM and rehabilitation group; and a usual care group.[8] The best results were found with the combination of Transcendental Meditation and rehabilitation. In this group, patients showed an average of 20.7% increase of blood flow to the brain. The researchers were not sure of the mechanism but speculated that "reduced levels of stress hormones and possible inflammation may improve the functioning of the cells lining the coronary arteries."[9]

Traumatic stress

Traumatic stress is a different story. It was difficult to believe that in the year 2022, a war was taking place in Europe, normally peaceful citizens were preparing Molotov cocktails, many were holding a gun for the first time in their lives, and scenes of destruction not witnessed since the 1990 Balkan Wars filled TV screens across the globe. If this was not a situation that created traumatic stress, it is difficult to know what was. Many victims died anonymously, and a large number of those going out to fight on both sides returned to their families with severe traumatic stress. Nowhere are the dangers of high levels of cortisol seen more than with these dreadful conditions. Nevertheless, recent research indicates the possibility of reducing the consequences of war stress.

According to the David Lynch Foundation's Center for Resilience, around one million military veterans experience post-traumatic stress and, shockingly, fewer than 20% of these will have received adequate care due to ineffective treatments, the eternal fear of stigma, and a lack of government resources. Post-traumatic stress has unpleasant consequences. It can severely limit the ability to function and can expose veterans to the dangers of severe depression, anxiety, alcohol and drug abuse, and emotional numbness. It brings with it the inability to participate in life and a loss of positive emotions such as happiness. Even more worryingly, it can also result in violent or self-destructive behavior or the release of intense emotional pain, including suicide.[10]

Nevertheless, the benefits of the Transcendental Meditation technique for reducing symptoms of PTS, such as stress, anxiety, depression, substance use disorder, and heart disease, have long been recognized in research studies, including randomized controlled trials. As highlighted by the Center for Resilience, the secret of the Transcendental Meditation program lies in the experience, gained with regular practice of the technique, of deep metabolic rest coupled with heightened mental alertness. This is a state known in scientific terms as "restful alertness," the mind/body component of Transcendental Consciousness, and is a powerful remedy for stress.

Stress and emotional intelligence

Overall, a wide range of studies indicates that reducing stress through practice of Transcendental Meditation affects many areas of human life including emotional intelligence, the ability to control and express our emotions, and the capacity to manage interpersonal relationships wisely and compassionately. In scientific terms, emotional intelligence is "the ability to perceive emotions in oneself and others, and to understand, regulate, and use such information in productive ways toward successful environmental adaptation and problem solving."[11]

The concept of emotional intelligence has gained considerable attention, especially in the workplace, because of its connections with mental and physical health and social-emotional aptitudes. Research findings indicate a significant decrease in perceived stress in practitioners of Transcendental Meditation as compared with controls, as well as a significant increase in emotional intelligence.[12] The question might be: "Why does this happen?"

It happens because Transcendental Meditation allows the mind to easily settle down and experience profound inner silence of abstract wakefulness, or Transcendental Consciousness, the quietest state of our awareness and an infinite reservoir of happiness, creativity, and intelligence. With experience of this reservoir, any doubts we may have that happiness is not built into the very nature of life are likely to disappear. When we come back into activity, we bring just a small amount of this field of happiness back with us, but every time we dive back in again and experience the transcendent, then the amount of inner happiness, inner bliss, increases in our awareness and our emotions.

The process of repeatedly diving into silence and coming out into activity is reflected in a very precious branch of the ancient Vedic literature of India. This branch is the Upanishad, which expresses the story of silence and how it is revealed in everyday things. The Chāndogya Upanishad, for instance, includes a narrative between a young boy and his father, in which the father explains the essence of truth. He notes that when people contact the deepest silence, "they become one with it and do not remember their individual natures. Yet when they are active, they again become a teacher, a farmer, or a goldsmith."[13] It is so simple. We are who we are, yet when we transcend, we become one with an infinite reservoir of peace and happiness. When we come back into activity, we are again who we are but with something added: a little more peace, and a little more happiness.

Chapter 7

The *Bhagavad Gītā* and the *Tao Te Ching*

Expansion of happiness is the purpose of creation.

Maharishi Mahesh Yogi[1]

If you like to walk or socialize with others, you are likely to encounter many different people in the process. They will look just like you, talk like you, and laugh as you do. You might be astonished, however, to know what percentage of them are quietly, in the privacy of their own homes, or behind closed doors in their offices, having deep experiences of transcending. Each person may call it by a different name: Samādhi, the Self, the Tao, Nirvana, the peace that passes all understanding, or Being. But however it is named, it is a fourth state of consciousness that is referred to in this book mostly as Transcendental Consciousness or the Self. Many people believe that to experience the transcendent they would need to abandon society and become a monk or a recluse. But those who experience Transcendental Consciousness do not need to live in the Himalayas. In fact, the number of people who are genuine recluses and prefer to live apart from the world is small. We each have to live our own truth, as William Shakespeare understood so well when he wrote, "This above all: to thine own self be true."[2] The recluse life is not for everyone, nor does it have to be for everyone. Most of us are destined to be social beings, living in communities, having families, and working together. That is where our life satisfaction comes from and to try to live a recluse life we are not suited for would only bring eventual confusion.

To understand Transcendental Consciousness better, two texts have influenced societies for millennia: the *Bhagavad Gītā* and the *Tao Te Ching*. The message of both texts is similar and profound: that the vast range of material creation is both brought into existence and permeated with the ocean of Transcendental Consciousness, a field of peace and bliss forever remaining beyond the realm of the intellect.

The *Bhagavad Gītā*

Maharishi Mahesh Yogi's commentary on the *Bhagavad Gītā* refers to Transcendental Consciousness mostly as the Self, the ground of all levels of life. There is, of course, a difference between the Self and the self, or the higher Self and the lower self. The lower self (lower-case s) is that aspect of our personalities that functions within the "relative," the ever-changing existence characterized by our waking, dreaming, and sleeping experiences. Basically, the lower self is the thinking mind, the deciding intellect, and our feelings or emotional state. The "Self" (upper-case S), on the other hand, is that part of our being that never changes and is the source of all relative existence including the human mind, intellect, and feelings. As Maharishi comments,

> The great words of enlightenment found in the Vedas express Being as the ultimate reality and find It within man as his own inseparable Self. They reveal the truth in the expressions: "I am That," "Thou art That," "All this is That," "That alone is," and "There is nothing else but That." In these expressions and many like them, which have been the source of inspiration and enlightenment to millions of people from time immemorial, the Indian philosophy expounds the oneness of life as the ultimate reality, absolute Being.[3]

The *Bhagavad Gītā* shows how we can become established in the abstract, absolute field of pure Being, the Self. Traditionally, reading the *Bhagavad Gītā* is said to take us from ignorance to wisdom and from suffering to happiness. It is a fundamental text of the Vedic tradition of knowledge cherished in India since times immemorial, and the heart of a great epic known as the Mahabharata. Although the Mahabharata is the story of two sets of cousins, the Pandavas and the Kauravas, and the conflict between them, it is really the teaching of eternal Truth, given by Lord Kṛishṇa to the hero of the text, Arjuna, on the battlefield of life as well as on the battlefield of an impending war.

The *Bhagavad Gītā* continually refers to the ultimate reality that lies beyond the field of the senses. One example comes from Chapter 2, Verse 45, which states, "The Vedas' concern is with the three Guṇas. Be without the three Guṇas, O Arjuna, freed from duality, ever firm in purity, independent of possessions, possessed of the Self."[4]

According to the Vedic tradition of knowledge, creation is the interplay of the three Guṇas, *Sattwa*, *Rajas*, and *Tamas*, the three tendencies of nature. Rajas is responsible for motion and energy. It is the spur to activity while Sattwa (purity) creates a new state and Tamas (darkness) destroys the old one. Sattwa, Rajas, and Tamas are always together in every state. They cannot be separated, as the function of each balances and complements the others.

As maintained by Maharishi, the phrase "Be without the three Gunas" is an instruction to go beyond the three forces of nature, in other words, relative everyday life and its endless stream of opposites, and experience the unchanging transcendent.[5] Everything in the changing world has an opposite: light and dark, night and day, hard and soft, conflict and peace, harmony and disharmony. The list goes on and on. Opposites pull in different directions so to go beyond the opposites is to find relief in an unchanging unity and peace.

The phrase "ever firm in purity" means remaining untainted by the faintest hint of relative activity and therefore being beyond the possibility of harming oneself, anyone else, or the environment. "Independent of possessions" does not necessarily mean abandoning all possessions but can be understood as not being bound by, or attached to, possessions, not craving what we do not have or being anxious to preserve what we already have. And finally, "possessed of the Self" means being immersed in the bliss of the Self, a state not as far away from us as we may think.[6] This is also the message of the *Tao Te Ching*.

The *Tao Te Ching*

Two thousand years ago, in ancient China, a series of profound principles were put in writing and attributed to a great sage, Lao Tzu. These principles are a guide to living a life of peace and compassion, which by inference leads to happiness. Lao Tzu describes Transcendental Consciousness in this way:

> It is unseen because it is colorless;
> it is unheard because it is silent;
> if you try to grasp it, it will elude you,
> because it has no form.
> Because of its diverse qualities
> it cannot be summarized,
> yet it comprises an essential unity.[7]

And he advises his followers to quieten the activity of their minds and seek the root, the source of life. If they do, then they will find tranquility.

> Seek composure—the essence of tranquility.
> All things are in process, rising and returning.
> Plants blossom for a season, then return to the root.
> In returning to the root, we find tranquility;
> this leads to our destiny, which is eternity.
> To know eternity is enlightenment.[8]

The following two quotes show the similarity in essence between Maharishi Mahesh Yogi's description of the Self (absolute Being), and the Tao.

Being is the unmanifested reality of all that exists, lives, or is. Being is the ultimate reality of all that was, is, or will be. It is eternal and unbounded, the basis of all the phenomenal existence of the cosmic life.[9]

The eternal Tao is unnamable.
In its simplicity it appears insignificant,
but the whole world cannot contain it.
If rulers would follow it,
their citizens would pay homage.
If the people would follow it,
they would have no need of rulers.
Earth and sky are made one by it,
forming sweet dew drops.
When the Tao expresses itself in creation,
it becomes visible.[10]

Here, the Tao is presented as both invisible in its ultimate reality and visible as it expresses itself in creation. Compare this with the description of pure Being, the Self, and the two seem as one. Both the *Bhagavad Gītā* and the *Tao Te Ching* are guides to successful living. The *Tao Te Ching* presents a deeply meaningful exposition of the life of the wise who aim to spontaneously create good with effortless skill by living in accord with the wisdom of the Tao, the fundamental reality of creation. Its central message is one of simplicity. This is expressed in principle number 7:

The wise humble themselves,
and because of their humility,
they are worthy of praise.

They put others first, and so become great.
They are not focused on outcomes or achievements,
therefore they always succeed.[11]

Simplicity is also central to the *Bhagavad Gītā*, which offers guidance on how to live through contact with the Self, the inner Being of all things.

The Self, the Tao, is not the province of any one meditation technique, any culture, or any religion. In its unfathomable depth, it is found everywhere in every great tradition and culture. Mentions or hints of it by other names even appear in many books including novels such as *The Secret Garden* by Frances Hodgson Burnett, written in 1911.

It was as if a sweet clear spring had begun to rise in a stagnant pool and had risen and risen until at last it swept the dark water away. But of course he did not think of this himself. He only knew that the valley seemed to grow quieter and quieter as he sat and stared at the bright delicate blueness. He did not know how long he sat there or what was happening to him, but at last he moved as if he were awakening and he got up slowly and stood on the moss carpet, drawing a long, deep, soft breath and wondering at himself. Something seemed to have been unbound and released in him, very quietly.[12]

Trying to make sense of our lives is not always easy. For practitioners of Transcendental Meditation, however, the process leads, almost inevitably, to the desire to understand the universe and our place in it. In many ways, practitioners are asking about the truth of reality, the reasons for life, freedom, and differences. In short, they are asking about consciousness, Transcendental Consciousness, other states of consciousness, and they have good reason to ask because consciousness involves experience and is fundamental to life.

From the moment we open our eyes from sleep, we experience the world with one or more of our five senses. The truth is that if there is no consciousness, no awareness, then there is no experience, and thus, no universe, no art, no science, no joy, no happy world. So, what is this mysterious thing we call consciousness?

Part II
Understanding Consciousness

Chapter 8

The Philosopher's View

The stream of knowledge is heading towards a non-mechanical reality; the Universe begins to look more like a great thought than like a great machine. Mind no longer appears to be an accidental intruder into the realm of matter ... we ought rather hail it as the creator and governor of the realm of matter.

James Jeans[1]

Do philosophers and scientists want to find meaning in human experience and create a happy world? The answer is probably yes to differing degrees. Philosophers aim to unify the different parts of our understanding. They consider ethics, human values, and the meaning of existence to deepen their (and our) understanding of life so that everyone can act from a platform of greater wisdom and enjoy a better quality of life. Scientists too aim to uncover truths about existence, truths about the universe, and truths about our place in the universe. They share insights with the public in the hope that their discoveries will improve the well-being and happiness not just of us, but also of societies in the future. But whatever insights philosophers and scientists generate are based on their personal, or collective, understanding of reality. They may ask: How does the brain produce consciousness? Do the neurons in the brain produce consciousness, or does consciousness produce the neurons? But the answers to these questions are interpreted by a factor other than purely objective perception. They are based on the worldview, or the state of consciousness, of the perceiver, and that worldview varies from one individual to another and from one generation to the next. That is why there are different

59

answers in both philosophy and science to the question: "What is consciousness?" The question is essential because our long-term happiness and well-being depend on it.

The elusive consciousness

Most current definitions of consciousness propose that consciousness is produced by the brain. But so far, none have convincingly explained how the brain's mechanisms give rise to subjective experiences such as feelings of happiness or love, if in fact they do. "Is love a fancy, or a feeling? No. It is immortal as immaculate Truth." Was this famous section of a poem by the English poet David Hartley Coleridge produced solely by unthinking neurons in the brain? Or did it come from the mind of a poet who saw something of the truth of life through the lens of his own consciousness? These are questions that have not yet been satisfactorily answered by scientists or philosophers.

Their views on knowledge are varied because they are dealing with something that seems abstract. The German philosopher Arthur Schopenhauer, often labeled a pessimist, held that "Every man takes the limits of his own field of vision for the limits of the world."[2] In other words, it is easy to think that because we cannot see something, it does not exist. Transcendental Consciousness is out of our field of vision and yet, according to the Upanishads so loved by Schopenhauer, "Ātmā [Transcendental Consciousness] is all there is."[3]

Most philosophers may think the mind is more than the brain but cannot accept the idea that the brain might be made of consciousness and not the other way around. To get to the point, there are three primary schools of thought: scientific materialism, dualism, and monism. Of course, each category has many subcategories, even sub-subcategories, but in the end, they boil down to one of these three main categories.

Scientific materialism

In earlier chapters, materialism was presented as a liking for material possessions at the expense of exploring a nonmaterial perspective where spiritual values are a significant part of the culture. "Scientific Materialism" as a philosophy, however, holds that at the end of the day, everything is physical. It shares many features with a form of philosophy called "physicalism," which, as the name suggests, maintains that the world, the universe, and everything in it—thoughts, feelings, experiences are physical, and consciousness is the result of physical processes. According to an article in *Philosophy Now*, extreme physicalists, or materialists, think that "distinct minds and experiences don't exist: there are only brains and their physical activities."[4] Physicalists might accept that there are some things that appear nonphysical, but when it comes down to it, they believe they must be physical at their source.[5]

Currently, most scientists seem to think that the physicalist view of life is correct. They agree that consciousness exists because with all the different subjective perceptions of the world, it would be hard to argue that it doesn't exist. Nevertheless, physicalists, those who believe that the world is entirely physical, have tried to establish their worldview as a normal commonsense perspective on life, but their reasoning cannot adequately explain the extraordinary range of subjective feeling. Subjective feeling includes all the different stages of happiness, everything from pure unadulterated happiness that lasts, to fleeting moments of happiness that vanish almost as soon as they appear.

The American philosopher Daniel Dennett, who shares the physicalist perspective, argues that our brain's ability to compute deceives us into thinking we understand consciousness. He insists that we don't, because as far as he is concerned, consciousness is the outcome of physical processes in our brains. He suggests that,

We're just made of cells, about 100 trillion of them. Not a single one of those cells is conscious; not a single one of those cells knows who you are, or cares. Somehow, we have to explain how when you put together teams, armies, battalions of hundreds of millions of little robotic unconscious cells — not so different really from a bacterium, each one of them — the result is this. I mean, just look at it. The content — there's color, there's ideas, there's memories, there's history. And somehow all that content of consciousness is accomplished by the busy activity of those hordes of neurons.[6]

Not everyone agrees with this materialist extremism. For author Grant Bartlett, editor of *Philosophy Now*, this idea is absurd.

If it were true as stated, you could not be having experiences, such as the experiences you're having now, and the perpetrators of this doctrine would have to claim themselves to be mindless zombies or automata, writing their books mindlessly. Even to say that experience is an *illusion* ignores the fact that a supposed 'illusion' of having an experience is still *having an experience*; and for an experience to exist, all that is necessary is that the experience is experienced, regardless of whatever else one might say about its nature or cause.[7]

Scientific materialism reduces everything to the physical. If this is true, then it means that everything we discover, everything we create, only has a meaning if we impose one on it and when we pass on, then our memories, our creativity, and our beliefs, are lost. The problem with scientific materialism is that it does nothing to further the need of people for a life that has significance. Yet significance exists in life, so can there be personal significance if such a quality is not built into the universe itself?

Dualism

While, according to the online *Free Dictionary*, the term "dualism" in philosophy refers to the view "that the world consists of or is explicable as two fundamental entities, such as mind and matter," the term "consciousness" stems from the Latin *con* (with) and *scire* (to know). The fact that consciousness is related to the ability to know, implies that we are aware, and aware of something. The 17th century French philosopher René Descartes, a proponent of dualism, was definitely aware of something when he coined the phrase *cogito ergo sum* (I think, therefore I am), meaning that if he was thinking, even if the thinking was wrong, he must exist. Descartes also believed that to establish the fundamental truths of metaphysics, the mind must be withdrawn from the senses because the senses are unreliable.[8]

> I would advise none to read this work, unless such as are able and willing to meditate with me in earnest, to detach their minds from commerce with the senses, and likewise to deliver themselves from all prejudice...[9]

Descartes' thinking was dualist in nature, signifying that he held every human mind to be a mental substance, and every body to be a part of one material substance [10] However, his reasoning was challenged by Princess Palatine Frederick (Elisabeth of Bohemia), the daughter of the exiled, poverty-stricken Queen of Bohemia. The letters between Descartes and Elisabeth are erudite, interesting, and expressive of a very deep friendship. In one of her early letters to Descartes, Elisabeth asks:

How can the soul of a man determine the spirits of his body so as to produce voluntary actions (given that the soul is only a think substance)? For it seems that all determination of movement is made by the pushing of a thing moved, either that it is pushed by the thing that moves it or it is affected by the quality or shape of the surface of that thing. For the first two conditions, touching is necessary for the third extension. For touching, you exclude entirely the notion that you have of the soul; extensions seem to me incompatible with an immaterial thing. This is why I ask you to give a definition of the soul more specific than the one you gave in your metaphysics.[11]

Fundamentally, Elisabeth is asking Descartes a question about the relationship between consciousness and matter. How can the soul move or affect the body if it is separate from the body? And how can our minds, attached to our physical bodies and imbued with all the moods, emotions, and desires that go with that body, achieve the stark level of reasoning necessary for pure objective knowledge? Elisabeth queries Descartes' belief in the separation of the mind from the body, in other words dualism, at a time when women were not expected to think about such concepts, let alone question them.

Monism

Whereas materialists such as Daniel Dennett think that the mind is ultimately physical, other philosophers disagree. Bernardo Kastrup, for instance, subscribes to idealism, a monistic philosophy that associates reality with mind rather than with material objects. In his book, *Why Materialism Is Baloney*, he states that "If idealism is correct, then mind is not within the brain, because it is the brain that is within mind."[12] He argues that our whole environment is constantly imposing views on us, whether it is the media, advertisements, political rhetoric, or documentaries. In fact, the current worldview that is consciously or subconsciously pushed on us is steeped in materialist philosophy.

> While acknowledging that there are many superficial worldviews operating simultaneously in society, there is a powerful core worldview that subtly pervades the deepest, often 'subconscious' levels of our minds, ultimately determining how we truly feel about ourselves and reality. This core worldview is materialism. Many of us absorb materialist beliefs from the culture without even being aware of it, all the while trusting that we hold other beliefs. Materialism suffuses the core of our being by a kind of involuntary osmosis. Like a virus, it spreads unnoticed until it's too late and the infection has already taken a firm hold.[13]

Kastrup champions the view that what we consider to be the cold reality of our lives is ungrounded and flies in the face of reason and observation.[14] His work leads the contemporary renaissance of what is referred to as metaphysical idealism, the idea that reality is essentially mental rather than material. For metaphysical idealists, the entire universe exists in mind, and mind gives rise to the configurations of matter and energy. The inference of this perspective is that everything one learns about the separateness of one mind from another is both true and false. On the face of it, our minds belong to us. We have our own thoughts and feelings, and they are not the same thoughts and feelings as those of our neighbors. Nevertheless, if "Mind" gives rise to all minds, then the source of all minds lies in one universal mind. To illustrate this principle, Kastrup makes a parallel with dissociative identity disorder, where a unified mind breaks down into multiple personalities. This is a way of understanding how one universal consciousness might become many different forms and phenomena.

British philosopher Philip Goff is another who doubts the worth of materialist philosophies and subscribes to a form of monism. He pinpoints an essential flaw in materialism by suggesting in his book *Galileo's Error* that if the concept of materialism were true, we would be able to know the color yellow simply by reading neuroscience. We would not need to have the experience of yellow. He then poses an interesting question.

The human brain is an extraordinarily complex organ, involving almost a hundred billion neurons each directly connected with ten thousand others, yielding some ten trillion nerve connections. But, you might reasonably wonder, where in those trillions of neural connections is Susan [a synonym for every human being]: her hopes and fears, pleasures and pains, the indefinable essence of her personality?[15]

Goff supports the idea of Panpsychism ("pan" meaning everything, and "psyche" meaning mind), which is the idea that consciousness is fundamental to physical reality. This does not mean that everything is "conscious" in the way that human beings are conscious; it simply means that consciousness exists in progressively simpler forms in less and less complex organisms. Additionally, Goff holds that Panpsychism is "more consonant with human happiness than rival views."[16] Bringing his view of consciousness into contact with everyday reality, he states:

Panpsychism has the potential to transform our relationship with the natural world. If Panpsychism is true, the rain forest is teeming with consciousness. As conscious entities, trees have value in their own right: chopping one down becomes an action of immediate moral significance. Moreover, on the

Panpsychist worldview, humans have a deep affinity with the natural world: we are conscious creatures embedded in a world of consciousness.[17]

At the end of *Galileo's Error*, he adds, "My hope is that Panpsychism can help humans once again to feel that they have a place in the universe. At home in the cosmos, we might begin to dream about—and perhaps make real—a better world."[18]

Chapter 9

A Scientist's View

The universe is entirely mental ... There have been serious [theoretical] attempts to preserve a material world—but they produce no new physics, and serve only to preserve an illusion.

Richard Conn Henry[1]

Some physicists have also supported the idea of a universal connection that flows throughout nature. For instance, theoretical physicist David Bohm noted "an underlying order and comprehensive connectivity, a unity to the cosmos, a wholeness not predicted by mere probability theory."[2] Mathematician and physicist Freeman Dyson stated, "Mind is inherent in the way the universe is built."[3] The German theoretical physicist Max Planck declared, "I regard consciousness as fundamental. I regard matter as derivative of consciousness."[4] Werner Heisenberg, one of the founders of quantum physics, suggested that the "frame [of materialism] was so narrow and rigid that it was difficult to find a place in the current framework of understanding for many concepts of our language that had always belonged to its very substance, for instance, the concept of mind, of the human soul or of life."[5] And British physicist, astronomer, and mathematician Sir James Jeans held that "The universe begins to look more like a great thought than like a great machine. Mind no longer appears as an accidental intruder into the realm of matter; we are beginning to suspect that we ought rather to hail it as the creator and governor of the realm of matter."[6]

If "mind" is not an accidental intruder into the realm of matter, but instead, the creator and governor of matter, then our sense of direction and purpose can be regained and, as human beings, we can feel that life is indeed intensely meaningful.

That in itself will bring greater happiness and fulfillment to a population starved of significance.

Mind or machine?

James Jeans queried the physical direction of science into a purely mechanical reality. He not only proposed that matter is continuously created throughout the universe, but also wrote books aiming to popularize his views. *The Mysterious Universe* is probably the best known of these. In the final chapter, he states: "If the universe is a universe of thought, then its creation must have been an act of thought. Indeed, the finiteness of time and space almost compel us, of themselves, to picture the creation as an act of thought."[7] Jeans is by no means in the majority in thinking that creation is an act of thought, but the concept certainly makes sense. Similar to the question whether there can be personal significance if significance is not built into life itself is the query: "Can human beings have intelligence if intelligence is not built into the very fabric of the universe?"

Harvard-trained quantum physicist John Hagelin, a scientist formerly at the European Center for Nuclear Research (CERN) and the Stanford Linear Accelerator (SLAC), argues that consciousness, or intelligence, is a fundamental property of the natural world. He suggests that there are features in common between pure consciousness, as the basis of the entire diverse creation, and the unified field of modern physics, the basis of the material universe from the perspective of physics. According to Hagelin, "The fundamental qualities of the unified field are the fundamental qualities of pure consciousness."[8] These qualities include intelligence, dynamism, and the ability to be self-referral, self-interacting, and self-aware.

By definition, the unified field of physics is purely self-interaction—the self-sufficient source of all created things. Similarly, pure consciousness is purely self-interacting, or "self-referral"—the self-sufficient source of all mental activity.

If these two fields are both purely self-interacting, and if they interact with one another (as, for example, the subjective mind and the material body ultimately must), then they must be one and the same.[9]

Hagelin, whose scientific input includes some of the most quoted references in the physical sciences, holds that "The unified field is a non-material, self-interacting, self-aware, dynamic field of intelligence, which is equivalent to saying that it is a field of universal consciousness. It has all the fundamental characteristics of consciousness."[10] In this model, all the fundamental characteristics of consciousness would include the ability of the field of consciousness to know itself and refer back to itself to determine its next action.

Moving toward unity

Intelligence engulfs the work of Italian neuroscientist Giulio Tononi who developed his Integrated Information Theory, a theoretical framework to understand consciousness. Tononi defines integrated information as "the amount of information generated by a complex of elements, above and beyond the information generated by its parts."[11] Currently, his Integrated Information Theory is the leading theory in neuroscience, which is interesting since it proposes that consciousness is the fundamental property of any physical system.[12] Tononi holds that every experience is unified and cannot be subdivided into its component parts, meaning that the left and right side, the color and the shape, everything about the experience is always one integrated information. An example of this is raising one hand. Such a simple act involves more possibilities of range, expression, tension, and direction than we can count in one lifetime, yet when we raise our hand, it is unique at that moment and perceived as a unified experience. In more expanded terms, one could sum up Tononi's Integrated Information Theory as: "The whole is more than the sum of its parts."

Dr. Fred Travis moves toward a unified experience from a different perspective. Having comprehensively studied the brain for several decades, he refers to brain functioning as an objective language that can give clear answers to abstract questions about human consciousness. He looks to the brain as a way of exploring the structure of inner subjectivity, a means to explore the vast range of individual consciousness, and a way of exploring how we are connected to the environment. Travis has conducted copious research on higher states of consciousness, especially experiences of Transcendental Consciousness. In 2005, he noted:

TM [Transcendental Meditation] practice appears to isolate self-awareness from the processes and content of experience. This experience of self-awareness, called Transcendental Consciousness, is subjectively characterized by the absence of the framework and content that define waking experiences. Physiologically, it is distinguished by apneustic breathing, autonomic orienting, and increases in the frequency of peak EEG power. When self-awareness is combined with perceptual and cognitive processes, through the agency of attention, conscious experience may result.[13]

This is a far greater move in the direction of a monistic view of consciousness, but can it go any further?

Chapter 10

Consciousness Is All There Is

The problems of our age are human problems. Crime, terrorism, drug dependency, even pollution result from failure to comprehend life's essential unity. The only way we can overcome these problems is through the expansion of consciousness.

John Hagelin[1]

In 2015, neuroscientist Tony Nader stated, "In all this uncertainty, one fact seems undeniable: the fact of our own awareness. Without awareness, we can neither perceive nor apprehend, neither see nor think nor dream. Commonly, this awareness is called consciousness."[2] Such a simple way of describing consciousness is something of a relief.

Tony Nader studied medicine at Harvard University and received his Ph.D. in neuroscience from Massachusetts Institute of Technology with the intention of ending suffering and discovering how the human mind and body function to guide people's behavior.[3] Early on, he recognized the great questions in life, the questions most of us ask at intervals, when we have the time to think about them, and have someone to bounce our thoughts off. As he comments:

I have devoted my life searching for answers, delving deeply into religious texts and their various interpretations and familiarizing myself with different schools of philosophy. It sometimes seemed to me as if people were living in their own different universes. I turned to the study of medicine, psychiatry and neurology to understand why, while being so similar, we can all be so different in our opinions, mindset, and points of view. How does the human nervous system produce the mind with its vagaries leading us to go in all directions...[4]

Nader is also a globally recognized Vedic scholar and head of the international Transcendental Meditation organizations in over 100 countries. Similarly to James Jeans, he holds that consciousness gives rise to the material universe and not the other way around.

> We start with a grand Axiom: There is one grand field of Consciousness that is completely non-physical and non-material. It is beyond time and space and therefore cannot be said to have a beginning or an end. The concept of something starting at some point in time and ending at another is valid in what we perceive as the physical and material realities. But it has no meaning in the absence of the physical and the material.[5]

Nader postulates that the very consciousness, on the ground of which human beings can experience, is fundamental to life, and he has put forward the idea of a field of consciousness that is not dependent on anything outside itself for its existence. Furthermore, he proposes that all manifestations originate within this field.[6]

If this is the case, then a field of "consciousness" is by definition conscious, and if it is conscious, it involves an observer, a process of observation, and something to observe, as conscious experience requires these three qualities. Since, in Nader's model, there is nothing outside the field of consciousness, the field itself must be its own observer, process of observation, and observed. While this may sound abstract, it simply means that the field being fully conscious of itself, or to put it another way, being fully "self-referral," observes itself through all the myriad processes of knowing that are also itself.

It sees itself and knows that it is everything, all the different shapes, sights, tastes, and sounds with different characteristics expressing different levels of consciousness. Indeed, without the three markers of consciousness—observer, process of observing, and the observed—nothing could exist including happiness because consciousness involves experience and no experience, no happiness, is possible without an observer, a process of observing, and something to be observed.[7]

Self-referral

For scientists such as Tony Nader, John Hagelin, and Fred Travis, a universal field of consciousness is fully self-referral, absolute and self-sufficient. It knows itself as a field of infinite possibilities and needs nothing outside itself to create those possibilities. Moreover, nothing, not one tiny particle, and everything the particle becomes, is outside the field of consciousness. That, therefore, is the vast, holistic, macroscopic view of consciousness, fully self-referral, unlimited, and universal. But what about the tiny, human, and not so universal, microscopic level?

In day-to-day life, to be self-referral as a human being is to look to our own feelings, needs, and intuitions, and be independent of outside pressures that make us behave in a way that is not our own. It is our ability to refer back to our own individual perceptions and experiences and for these perceptions and experiences to become the driving force behind what we do next. A simple example is seen in art. When an artist creates, the finished work is not divorced from the artist. Artistic creation is an extension of the artist's consciousness; it is a process of repeating, on a smaller scale, the ability of the macroscopic field of consciousness to refer back to itself to determine its next action. The artist too, consciously or unconsciously, refers back to the wholeness of their inner perceptions and experiences to create a work that expresses these inner experiences.

Similarly to Panpsychists who would agree that while everything *expresses* some aspect of consciousness, not everything is *conscious*, we could say that while everything has some degree of consciousness, not everything can refer back to itself to determine its next action. The point is that if pure consciousness is the ultimate constituent of creation, even a rock expresses some incredibly primitive form of consciousness and reacts to various elements such as light or heat without being aware that it is doing so. This is in contrast to the human mind that exists in a vast array of levels of consciousness, ranging from complete dullness to complete freshness, and can, to differing degrees, reflect on its own actions and feelings in a way that the humble rock cannot. Summing up, everything is consciousness, but not everything is conscious with the ability to be self-referral, the ability to look to itself before expressing its next action. Certainly not the rock.

A deeper understanding of consciousness

Consciousness is still a mystery to Western thinking, but not so much to Eastern thinking, particularly in India. The Indian subcontinent has a rich heritage of knowledge collected in what is known as the Vedic Literature, an integrated body of knowledge held by millions to be the most ancient and profound knowledge known to humanity. Advaita Vedānta, for instance, is a branch of the Vedic Literature. One of its texts, the Yoga Vasistha, states, "The world-appearance arises only when the infinite consciousness sees itself as an object."[8] This is a macrocosmic perspective of a very human perspective. When we wake after sleep, usually we are simply aware of ourselves coming awake. Only then does our awareness turn to all the details of ourselves, our room, and our world. Again, the Yoga Vasistha states, "When, in the infinite consciousness, the consciousness becomes aware of itself as its own object, there is the seed of ideation."[9]

The field of consciousness is its own observer, process of observation, and observed. That is not to say that the field of consciousness divides itself into three; the observer, the process of observation, and the observed are merely different aspects of consciousness. Basically, one becomes three, and three becomes multiplicity, a concept also reflected in the *Tao Te Ching*.

The Tao produces unity;
unity produces duality;
duality produces trinity;
trinity produces all things.[10]

For Maharishi Mahesh Yogi, everything, all forms of speech, actions, and even emotions are fluctuations of consciousness. Maharishi spent thirteen years of complete focus on gaining enlightenment with his own great teacher, Swami Brahmananda Saraswati, at the time Shankarāchārya of Jyotir Math in India.[11] Swami Brahmananda Saraswati was celebrated and loved by his followers for the knowledge he had and for the direct path to fulfillment he introduced. His primary wish was that all people, regardless of culture or background, should realize eternal truth and complete fulfillment. Maharishi shared that desire. For him, as with other great visionaries, consciousness is fundamental to life, the essence and substance of life, and the source of all time, space, causation, and happiness.[12] He also holds that the holistic field of Transcendental Consciousness is aware of itself as a wholeness in the same way that we are aware of ourselves as a wholeness. Put simply, however much we change, there is still a sense of "I." Hence, to offer a final definition, consciousness, or wakefulness, can be described as a state of knowingness, a state where the macroscopic universal field of consciousness knows itself fully, and, on a smaller, microscopic level, we are conscious of ourselves and our environment to whatever extent we can be.

In the next three chapters, we will look at human development, from infancy to adulthood, and the different stages of development that growth of human consciousness travels through. The point is that with the passage of time and attention, human consciousness, if accepted as a state of knowingness, can change and grow ... and achieve greater and greater states of happiness.

Chapter 11

Developing Happiness

The key to growth is the introduction of higher dimensions of consciousness into our awareness.

Lao Tzu[1]

For millennia, human beings have looked outward to the stars to try to fathom the far reaches of the universe. NASA's latest Webb Space Telescope, for example, is capable of revealing detailed full-color images of the universe never before seen. It will record images of the Carina Nebula, one of the brightest nebulae in the sky, located approximately 7,600 light-years away and home to massive stars larger than our sun. Even further away at about the 290 million light-years range is Stephan's Quintet, consisting of five galaxies. Located in the constellation Pegasus, four out of five of Stephan's galaxies are "locked in a cosmic dance of repeated close encounters."[2] The idea that we will be able to watch this dance through the latest imagery is extremely exciting. In the same way we thirst for greater understanding of the universe, we also seek more knowledge about our own experiences and our development as human beings. Changing perceptions take place all the time in what are termed the three "relative" states of consciousness: waking, dreaming, and sleeping. With sleeping, we are unaware of the world, yet sleep is necessary because it gives rest to the mind and body. Dreaming also serves a purpose. Evidence suggests that dreams allow "emotional processing and regulation" and could help process stressful events.[3] Waking naturally needs no explanation other than to say that when we are awake, we perceive life as changing, and we change with it. Events come and go; we see siblings and friends who shared our early experiences grow up and develop different lives. Our tastes alter, the things we want to do alter, the food we eat and the life choices we make transform. We gain a more complex appreciation of the world and a wider capability for happiness. Thus, change is the operative word when it comes to relative states of consciousness.

In our everyday world, we reach for happiness in whatever way we can—relationships, wealth, power—but moments of happiness experienced in these states have a habit of exploding in euphoric bubbles and then leaving us alone or as we were before. It is not surprising, therefore, that believing that permanent happiness is monotonous or uncomfortable to be around makes some people distrust happiness. It is understandable, but the happiness discussed in this book is the gradual but steady growth of life satisfaction that eventually continues throughout the challenges as well as the successes of our actions. It begins in the sensorimotor stage of babyhood and carries us forward into higher states of consciousness, the transformation of mind, body, and perception into a happiness that is so much more than anything of the everyday. Speaking an obvious truth, how we are is reflected in how we see the world and how we act in it. As described by Maharishi Mahesh Yogi:

The art of action is such that, although the doer is fully identified with the thought of the work, the process of action, and the enjoyment of the fruit of his action, he yet remains in the state of eternal freedom, saturated in bliss consciousness of absolute Being. So the art of action requires that Being be saturated into the nature of the mind and, through it, be brought to express the world of forms and phenomena.[4]

For Maharishi, our everyday waking state knowledge is immature because the things we think we know cannot be relied upon. The sun does not go around the earth, the earth travels around the sun. A wave can be a particle and a particle can be a wave. Electrons are "here" and "there" simultaneously. In fundamental physics, nothing is what it seems. Similarly with life: we can know someone for 30 years and still be surprised by them. The ever-present dangers of stress can overshadow the human mind and distort both perception and analysis of perception.[5] But, on the positive side, increasing our perception to facilitate greater understanding of the world not only makes us happier and of more help to our friends and environment, but is also a necessary part of human development.

The human mind with its enormous range is conscious of itself, its needs, and its environment. It can reason, remember, interpret, feel happiness and love, and have a sense of self, many of these activities operating simultaneously. Our minds consist of multiple levels extending from the most expressed to the least expressed level. For instance, the five senses interpret the sense data entering our awareness; the conscious thinking mind, being more subtle, reasons and identifies; the intellect, more subtle still, distinguishes and decides; the feeling level, yet more abstract, exists in the background but can be highly influential in terms of our reactions and behavior; and the ego, the experiencer, aware of its own identity, is the "I" that continues throughout life from babyhood to old age. Beyond the ego is the level described by Maharishi as Transcendental Consciousness, completely silent, unbounded, and alert, where individual consciousness has expanded to its unbounded status.[6]

Stages of human development

In the past, children were thought of as small adults, but the Swiss psychologist and genetic epistemologist Jean Piaget changed this perspective.[7] Piaget revolutionized the way that we understand child development and established a theory of normal intellectual development from infancy through adulthood. His work revealed that the way children and young people think in terms of thinking, judging, and knowing is different from the ways adults think. In addition, he held that there are four fundamental stages of intellectual (cognitive) development:[8]

Sensorimotor: From birth to somewhere between 18 months and two years

In this early stage, infants focus only on what they see and do. They have physical interactions with their close surroundings and constantly experiment, finding out how their environment reacts. Later during this period, they realize that toys, etc. still exist even if they can't be seen, a sure sign of developing memory. As babies begin to crawl and then walk upright, their increasing mobility results in further cognitive development. Finally, the beginnings of language herald the end of the Sensorimotor stage and the start of the Preoperational phase.

Preoperational: From around two years to approximately seven years

In this stage, language develops as does memory and imagination. Young children start to understand cause and effect, see the difference between past and future, and engage in make-believe.

Concrete operational: From ages seven to 11

Here, concrete, logical reasoning grows. Children are able to think less about themselves and be more awake to outer events. They also discover that their thoughts and feelings may not be shared by their friends and family.

Formal operational: From adolescence (12 years upward) through adulthood

In the final stage of development, a stage that can last throughout life according to Piaget, young people can think in an abstract manner. Science, for instance, can be appreciated, as can algebra. Young people can generate their own theories and think about justice, possibilities, and relationships.

These are average ages and are not necessarily fixed because children and teens progress through the stages at different ages and even demonstrate features of other stages at a given time. However, according to Piaget, intellectual or cognitive development always follows this same fourfold sequence. Some have questioned Piaget's theory; as they point out, culture and social environment can affect cognitive development. Nevertheless, Piaget's theory is widely accepted.

It is our perception and knowledge of our environment, namely our reality, that changes in Piaget's sequential stages of development. The change is from babyhood, where our world centers around close physical contacts and toys, through discovering that we may have different feelings from our siblings, to adulthood, where we have a better grasp of emotions and logic. That is how we develop, but it is not the sum total of our development. Our knowledge of the world is structured in our state of consciousness, and our state of consciousness determines how awake or aware we are to reality. That is why different people have such different views of life. We see the world through the lens of our own individual consciousness, and it may be different from our friend's state of consciousness. Indeed, how much of the total reality of life we understand is entirely dependent on our state of consciousness.

Many people have experiences of higher states of consciousness. They may not know that higher states exist or that they are experiencing a higher state, but they are doing so all the same. Even novelists have written about experiences of a higher consciousness without any knowledge of the phases of development that higher states progress through. Think of Frances Hodgson Burnett as she wrote in *The Secret Garden*: "He only knew that the valley seemed to grow quieter and quieter as he sat and stared at the bright delicate blueness,"[9] or the novelist Anya Seton who described a world of meaning in her classic novel *Katherine*:

> As she walked out into the little churchyard, it seemed lit with beauty. She stood bemused in a corner by a dark yew tree and saw meaning, blissful meaning, in everything her eye rested on: the blue floweret of the speedwell, the moss on a gravestone, an ant that labored to push a crumb through the grass—all these were radiant, as though she looked at them through crystal.[10]

The universality of experience

The British zoologist David Hay, after examining the results of an earlier survey, reported in his book *Something There* that religious or spiritual experiences were reported by 76% of the people who took part in the survey.[11] These results suggest that anyone can have transcendental experiences. Anyone can experience the parting of the curtain that hides deeper levels of reality so that a world we had not thought existed is seen glowing with bliss and immense meaning. With the growth of higher states, a new understanding of the world dawns. Over time, this deeper understanding extends to embrace the entirety of reality, not as a temporary flash of insight but as a permanent experience in life. The quality of fulfillment through gaining higher states of consciousness is addressed by Maharishi in the following quote:

> In evolution [of higher states of consciousness], life grows in steps of fulfillment and the person continually goes from more to even more and still more fulfillment. In the higher

stages of fulfillment is the joy of life and strength. We call this inner fulfillment the integration of life, because mind and body act in full co-operation and co-ordination.[12]

The mind becomes clearer and calmer as higher states of consciousness grow, and we are in a better position to assess the value of any knowledge put in front of us, better at discerning what is real from what is not real, better at being ourselves and not influenced by outside pressures, opinions, and beliefs. Our compassion for, and empathy with, others grows. We see the best in others and our ability to love increases. Bliss increases. Happiness increases. Recognition of meaning and purpose in life increases. If we develop these attributes to whatever degree, then we have more to offer to our families and our world.

Chapter 12

Spiritual Experience

Reality cannot be found except in one single source, because of the interconnection of all things with one another.

Gottfried Leibnitz[1]

According to Maharishi's model of human development, there are seven states of consciousness, which are listed below together with their Sanskrit names. Taken together, they indicate the unlimited range of the evolution of consciousness and the development of humanity, far beyond what is taught in schools today.

1	Waking	Relative state	*Jāgrat Chetanā*
2	Dreaming	Relative state	*Swapna Chetanā*
3	Sleeping	Relative state	*Sushupti Chetanā*
4	Transcendental Consciousness	Bridge to higher states of consciousness	*Turīya Chetanā*
5	Cosmic Consciousness	Higher state (still duality)	*Turīyātīt Chetanā*
6	Refined Cosmic (God) Consciousness	Higher state (still duality)	*Bhagavad Chetanā*
7	Unity Consciousness	Unified state of consciousness	*Brāhmī Chetanā*

Maharishi's model of higher states of consciousness

The most familiar states of consciousness experienced by the mind are waking, dreaming, and sleeping. Just to repeat, with deep sleep, there is usually no awareness at all; all knowledge has disappeared. When we dream, knowledge is illusory and cannot be trusted; the tiger pounces in the dream; it seems real and creates anxiety. But when we wake up, we know the tiger for what it is, or to put it in its most physical form, emotional content directly related to the level of activation in the amygdala.[2,3] The point is that our dreams seem real at the time, but in general, they are not. Any knowledge we have while dreaming needs to be carefully examined.

The waking state needs no introduction. No one would be reading this book if they were not awake. Unfortunately, once again, knowledge in the waking state cannot be considered reliable as events seem very different when experienced with a sharp, clear mind as opposed to a cloudy, tired, or depressed mind. In addition, things that do not interest us at one stage of our development assume significance at another stage. This shift can bewilder those close to us, but we change, and our interests and perspectives change. Thus, with waking, dreaming, and sleeping, any knowledge we receive has a somewhat limited value, but this is not the case with higher states, beginning with Transcendental Consciousness.

Transcendental Consciousness, the fourth state of consciousness

As explained earlier, Transcendental Consciousness is understood to be the universal field of consciousness, fundamental to life, and the source of the infinite diversity of creation. It can never be fully defined in a world of causation as it is beyond time and space yet gives rise to time and space. However, many have offered descriptions that go a long way toward helping our understanding of it. For instance, according to Maharishi Mahesh Yogi,

Transcendental Consciousness is bliss consciousness. When bliss consciousness comes within the range of the conscious mind, the mind is contented. On the platform of contentment, based on the positive experience of bliss, all the virtues flourish. Love, kindness, compassion, tolerance, appreciation of others, all naturally take hold of the mind...[4]

Kindness, compassion, tolerance, and appreciation of others are much loved qualities wherever we are because they make life more bearable in troubled times as well as good times. One kind word can make many friends. One cold word, spoken at a time of suffering, can drive them away.

In simple terms, great people like Maharishi came to the West because they saw a difference between the ideal of life in fulfillment and life as it was experienced by many who were suffering. Maharishi himself remained in the West to bring the knowledge and experience of fulfillment to as many people as possible, and began to teach Transcendental Meditation, a technique that not only gives the experience of peace and happiness to practitioners across the planet, but also supports the growth of higher states of consciousness.

This [Transcendental Consciousness] is a state of inner wakefulness with no object of thought or perception, just pure consciousness aware of its own unbounded nature. It is wholeness, aware of itself, devoid of differences, beyond the division of subject and object — transcendental consciousness. It is a field of all possibilities, where all creative potentialities exist together, infinitely correlated but as yet unexpressed. It is a state of perfect order, the matrix from which all the laws of nature emerge.[5]

This is a very different understanding from the idea that consciousness is produced by the brain. In fact, the two ways of thinking about consciousness could not be more dissimilar. In mainstream science, the brain produces consciousness. In mainstream spirituality, consciousness produces the brain. It is possible that scientists and philosophers might be more sympathetic to this latter perspective if they had more experiences of Transcendental Consciousness. Certainly, Plato must have had such experiences, as his description, in its beauty and simplicity, highlights the wholeness of Transcendental Consciousness.

Nor will his vision of the beautiful take the form of a face, or of hands, or of anything that is of flesh. It will be neither words nor knowledge, nor something that exists in something else, such as a living creature, or the earth, or the heavens, or anything that is—but subsisting of itself and by itself in an eternal oneness, while every lovely thing partakes of it in such sort that, however much the parts may wax and wane it will be neither more nor less, but still the same inviolable whole.[6]

Much later, theoretical physicist David Bohm also suggested the necessity of looking "on the world as an undivided whole, in which all parts of the universe, including the observer and his instruments, merge and unite in one totality."[7] And the great German poet and philosopher Johann Wolfgang von Goethe wrote:

How yearns the solitary soul
To melt into the boundless whole,
And find itself again in peace!
The blind desire, the impatient will,
The restless thoughts and plans are still;
We yield ourselves—and wake in bliss.[8]

Transcendental Consciousness through the ages
Transcendental Consciousness is far from being a new phenomenon; it has been spoken of throughout time. The great Indian sage Shankara advised his followers that "Transcending

every visible object of sense, fixing the mind on pure being, the totality of bliss, with right intentness within and without, pass the time while the bonds of action last."[9] Marcus Aurelius, stoic philosopher and emperor of Rome from 161 to 180 CE, noted, "Let thy intelligence also now be in harmony with the intelligence which embraces all things. For the intelligent power is no less diffused in all parts and pervades all things for him who is willing to draw it to him than the aerial power for him who is able to respire it."[10] And the transcendent is embedded in every verse of the *Tao Te Ching*:

The great Tao is everywhere!
It is on both the right and the left.
All things rely upon it for their existence,
and it sustains them.
It draws praise, but is not proud.
It lovingly nourishes everything,
and is not possessive.
It desires nothing, and so it is considered small.
Yet everything returns to it,
and so it should be considered great.[11]

The 13th century German theologian Meister Eckhart observed, "All that a man has externally in multiplicity is intrinsically One. Here all blades of grass, wood and stone, all things are One."[12] And as ever, attempts to describe the indescribable are found in poetry. Alfred Lord Tennyson was no exception to this. In his poem *The Ancient Sage*, he wrote:

More than once when I
Sat all alone, revolving in myself
The word that is the symbol of myself,
The mortal limit of the Self was loosed,
And passed into the nameless, as a cloud

Melts into heaven. I touch'd my limbs, the limbs
Were strange, not mine—and yet no shade of doubt,
But utter clearness, and thro' loss of Self
The gain of such large life as matched with ours
Were sun to spark—unshadowable in words,
Themselves but shadows of a shadow-world.[13]

In his early twenties, Schopenhauer began to use the term "better consciousness" to signify a consciousness that lies beyond reason and experience. He wanted something "greater than reason and rationality,"[14] and wrote, "The better consciousness in me lifts me into a world where there is no longer personality and causality or subject or object. My hope and belief are that this better (supersensible and extra-temporal) consciousness will become my only one."[15]

Experiences of the transcendent are beyond words, yet the feeling of many is to try to capture something of it—hence the poetry of Goethe, Marcus Aurelius, and Tennyson. We have the ability to experience Transcendental Consciousness through techniques such as the Transcendental Meditation technique and its advanced programs. The only thing we need to do is take our attention from the surface thinking level of the mind to the field of Transcendental Consciousness lying beyond all thinking and feeling.

One has only to allow the mind to move spontaneously from the gross field of objective experience, through the subtle fields of the thought-process to the ultimate transcendental Reality of existence. As the mind moves in this direction, it begins to experience increasing charm at every step until it reaches the state of transcendental bliss-consciousness.[16]

With the charm of transcendental experiences, the sense increases that human life has significance and can rise to higher states of consciousness with all their attendant benefits. These include living life with fewer mistakes and without fear. Living without fear is due to contact with bliss, and if we feel bliss, it is because Transcendental Consciousness is a field of bliss, and happiness reflects some level of it. A verse of the Taittirīya Upanishad, a branch of the Vedic tradition of knowledge, states:

> Surely by grasping the essence, one is filled with bliss.
> Who indeed would breathe, who would be alive
> if this bliss did not pervade space?
> For this essence alone bestows delight.[17]

Verifying Transcendental Consciousness

Different states of consciousness have their own distinct "signature" in the physiology. With sleep, body temperature drops and the brain's electrical activity changes as trillions of nerve cells within the brain are rewired. With dreaming, rapid eye movement (REM) takes place coupled with a loss of almost all muscle tone except for the diaphragm and eye muscles. And with waking, breathing is faster as is the heart rate, which circulates more oxygen via the blood. Transcendental Consciousness too has its own physiological signature, since specific EEG research can distinguish transcendental experiences from other experiences taking place during meditation. Instances of Transcendental Consciousness are distinguished by: a) significantly lower breath rates; b) high-frequency heart rate variability; c) increased electrical power in the 8–10 cycles per second alpha-1 frequency; and d) higher alpha coherence in the frontal regions of the brain.[18] Moreover, Fred Travis (see Chapter 2) holds that the experience of Transcendental Consciousness "should not be isolated to a few individuals transcending during meditation practice. Rather, the experience of Transcendental Consciousness should be available to everyone to allow them to realize their full human birthright."[19]

In the end, it is the steady practice of a technique such as Transcendental Meditation, that, over time, brings about the gradual buildup of bliss. To begin with, we simply start to feel more at peace and less overshadowed by difficulties, rather like having an internal armor that protects us from the challenges of our times. But however pleasant this sounds, experiences of Transcendental Consciousness are not the end goal. When Transcendental Consciousness is permanently maintained throughout waking, dreaming, and sleeping, then we gain a new state, the state known in the Vedic tradition as Cosmic Consciousness.

Chapter 13

Cosmic Consciousness and Above

Within man is the soul of the whole; the wise silence; the universal beauty, to which every part and particle is equally related; the eternal ONE.

Ralph Waldo Emerson[1]

Growth of Cosmic Consciousness through Transcendental Meditation practice is a little bit like the old method of dyeing cloth. Each time, the cloth is immersed in the dye and then placed in the sun. The sun fades it, but not as much as the time before or the time before that. There comes a moment when the dye is fast, and the sun no longer fades it. The cloth is ready to shine. It is the same thing with meditation. We experience transcendence as the mind dives beyond the thinking process and we bring something of that peace back when the mind comes back to the thinking level. With regular practice, the peace of the transcendent stays with us more and more until, over time, it is permanently established in our awareness. Once this happens, we cannot be shaken or disturbed by events no matter what they are. As Maharishi comments:

> The reward of bringing the mind to this state is that the small individual mind grows to the status of the cosmic mind, rising above all its individual shortcomings and limitations. It is like a small businessman becoming wealthy and reaching the status of a multimillionaire. The losses and gains of the market, which before used to influence him, now have no effect on him and he rises quite naturally above their influence.[2]

The only procedure necessary to gain Cosmic Consciousness is for our awareness to swing between the eyes-closed silence of Transcendental Consciousness and the eyes-open dynamism of activity, back and forth like breathing. The deep rest gained each time we dive within allows stress to be dissolved so that our nervous systems become increasingly flexible and capable of maintaining Transcendental Consciousness in activity. Thus, the sequence is this: Transcendental Meditation practitioners experience the profound silence of Transcendental Consciousness during meditation. Simultaneously, the metabolism, including our breathing and heart rate, settles down. We gain a state of "restful alertness" which, on the physical level, corresponds to Transcendental Consciousness. After meditation, we think and act and the silence fades. The process is repeated day after day, and each time, a little more silence and a little more happiness remain, until finally, each are permanently maintained even in deep sleep. This is Cosmic Consciousness. As Maharishi noted:

> In the state of highest evolution, in the field of Cosmic Consciousness, when the mind is brought to the fullest degree of the infusion of absolute Being, by nature the mind functions on the plane of purity in accordance with the natural laws engaged in carrying out the eternal process of evolution of everything in creation.[3]

Verifying Cosmic Consciousness

Studies on Cosmic Consciousness are beginning to emerge as more people either have temporary experiences of the state or are permanently established in it. One such study notes that "meditation-naïve" subjects (people who don't yet practice meditation) "exhibited lower consciousness-factor scores and lower frontal EEG coherence" while individuals reporting experiences of Cosmic Consciousness "exhibited higher consciousness-factor scores and higher frontal coherence."[4]

Physiological measures of these same subjects were also assessed.

> An electroencephalogram was recorded during simple and choice-paired reaction-time tasks. Each reaction-time task included a warning stimulus, a 1.5 s blank screen, and a second stimulus requiring a response. The brain preparatory response (contingent negative variation) was calculated before the second stimulus in both the simple and choice reaction-time tasks, and EEG patterns of power and coherence were calculated during the choice reaction-time tasks. During these challenging computer tasks, the subjects reporting Cosmic Consciousness, in comparison to subjects in the other two control groups, exhibited higher levels of broadband frontal EEG coherence (F3–F4), higher frontal and central relative power, and a better match in brain preparatory response to task demands during the simple and choice reaction-time tasks.[5]

The inner condition of Cosmic Consciousness, while it is held to be a state of complete inner happiness, is beyond transient expressions of fulfillment common to day-to-day living. Maharishi comments that no sorrow can enter that fulfillment, nor can the bliss of Cosmic Consciousness know "any gain greater than itself" since Cosmic Consciousness "leaves one steadfast in oneself, fulfilled in eternal contentment."[6]

Witnessing

One of the principal characteristics of Cosmic Consciousness is the experience of "witnessing," where our inner Self is experienced as being separate from activity. To put it another way, we are wrapped in a silence that is beyond time and space, quietly watching events unfold. One clarification is that the ordinary meanings of "witnessing" or "watching" suggest a connection or perceptual interaction between two or more events. In Cosmic Consciousness, however, our own unboundedness and the boundaries of our individual life in time and space coexist peacefully but without any connection between them. In other words, in Cosmic Consciousness, we are an unbounded witness to our own individual life, serenely witnessing our own activities and untouched by the comings and goings around us.

Witnessing can also be experienced during sleep and is another measure for scientists who wish to identify Cosmic Consciousness. Subjectively, witnessing during activity or sleep is assessed through individual self-reports. Objectively, research on witnessing consists of measuring the EEG tracings of those reporting witnessing during sleep.

Findings included EEG tracings of theta alpha (7–9 Hz) simultaneously with delta during deep sleep stages 3 and 4, decreased chin EMG, and highly significant increased theta2 and alpha1 relative power during stages 3 and 4 sleep as compared to controls.[7]

In one survey, 8% of a group of 235 volunteer students and staff at Maharishi International University (MIU), all of whom were practicing Transcendental Meditation and an advanced TM program, reported regular clear experiences of Transcendental Consciousness during sleep. Forty percent recorded experiences once a week or sporadically, 27% recorded having the experience once or twice, and 17% reported either vague or no experiences of witnessing deep sleep.[8] This might seem extraordinary but the kinds of experiences they were having are summed up in this example:

Often during dreaming, I am awake inside, in a very peaceful, blissful state. Dreams come and go, thoughts about the dreams come and go, but I remain in a deeply peaceful state, completely separate from the dreams and the thoughts.[9]

It looks a little like lucid dreaming until the experiencer's sense of Self is taken into consideration: "I remain in a deeply peaceful state, completely separate from the dreams and the thoughts." A very blissful state indeed, and development of higher states does not stop there.

Refined Cosmic Consciousness (God Consciousness)

While it would seem that Cosmic Consciousness completes the progression of states of consciousness, it is not the ultimate goal of human development. Cosmic Consciousness is the basis for the growth of further states, the next being a sixth state known as refined Cosmic Consciousness or God Consciousness.

Development toward refined Cosmic Consciousness is guided by the heart, which cannot bear separation between the profound inner silence of unchanging Transcendental Consciousness, and the relative, the entire field of change, or to put it another way, between Self and non-Self—as we experience in Cosmic Consciousness. The heart rises in waves of love, not on the level of mood-making, which is straining to feel something we don't feel, but on the level of sincere deep love for others. And, as the ability to love grows, perception of the world becomes more refined and delicate. In the state of refined Cosmic Consciousness, our attention no longer falls on the flaws of situations or even of other people, but on the softer, subtler values, the deeper structure, or inner reality of the objective world. In the waking state, we may not see the softer and more beautiful structure, but it is there, and it opens to our perception in, and on the way to, refined Cosmic Consciousness. Expansion of love and appreciation of others is directly associated with the experience of that deeper reality of life, the inner and more glorious reality that enriches the perception of the surface values and which was not available to us before.

Life becomes imbued with meaning and purpose as the most refined emotions of love and devotion take over and increase our sense of awe at creation itself. For instance, the German composer Ludwig van Beethoven may or may not have been in a high state of consciousness, but his experience of subtle values of perception was decidedly refined. When he finished his Symphony No. 7, part of which was used in the movie *The King's Speech*, he wrote: "Almighty One, in the woods I am blessed. Happy everyone in the woods. Every tree speaks through thee. O God! What glory in the woodland! On the heights is peace— peace to serve Him."[10] And the American writer and short story novelist Margaret Prescott Montague reported:

I cannot now recall whether the revelation came suddenly or gradually; I only remember finding myself in the very midst of those wonderful moments, beholding life for the first time in all its young intoxication of loveliness, in its unspeakable joy, beauty, and importance. I cannot say exactly what the mysterious change was. I saw no new thing, but I saw all the usual things in a miraculous new light—in what I believe is their true light. I saw for the first time how wildly beautiful and joyous, beyond any words of mine to describe, is the whole of life. Every human being moving across that porch, every sparrow that flew, every branch tossing in the wind, was caught in and was a part of the whole mad ecstasy of loveliness, of joy, of importance, of intoxication of life.

It was not that for a few keyed-up moments I imagined all existence as beautiful, but that my inner vision was cleared to the truth so that I saw the actual loveliness which is always there, but which we so rarely perceive.[11]

While we don't know what goes on in someone else's mind, phrases such as these seem to be natural expressions of experiences in refined Cosmic Consciousness. Appreciation of the environment expands to such an extent that love is experienced for every tiny pebble or distant star. Such a level of heartfelt love cannot be artificially created. When an experience like this comes, it is a natural appreciation for the more glorious depth of life, which now reveals itself on the surface. The inner life and light is now seen as the true reality and gives the world a new and extraordinary beauty. It's not simply greater love and appreciation as we might experience in ordinary perception; it's the perception of the finer and ultimately finest value of creation, even on the surface level of life, that gives rise to that greater love.

Self-reports of individuals who have had experiences of refined Cosmic Consciousness indicate that finer values are perceived on the surface value of the object of perception, which now becomes more intimate and the focus of deep appreciation. In describing the blissful nature of the sixth state of consciousness, Maharishi wrote that:

> Every perception, the hearing of every word, the touch of every little particle, and the smell of whatever it may be, brings a tidal wave of the ocean of eternal bliss—in every arising of a thought, word, or action is the arising of the tide of bliss.[12]

When refined Cosmic Consciousness, or God Consciousness, is finally established, our experience of the world is transformed. We experience the world in terms of its deeper, richer inner structure, which in turn allows us to be more effective in responding to the needs of the time. Greater and deeper love, springing from such a transformed state, allows for, and promotes, powerful, life-supporting action that can help to improve the world for others. Yet, even here, there is room for further development.

Unity Consciousness

When love for all things is full and complete, the gulf between the universal Self, the inner reality of our lives, and the seeming "other" finally melts away and the full range of creation is open to our perception. Even the most subtle value of creation is appreciated in terms of its infinite value and the full and complete reality of Unity Consciousness dawns.

> The intensity of this Union cultures man's consciousness, which begins to find everything inseparable from the Self; and this is how, in the most natural manner, the Self, which held Its identity as separate from all activity in the state of Cosmic Consciousness, finds everything in Itself.[13]

This is Unity Consciousness, where the inner, or transcendental, Self of the individual is experienced as unbounded and the inner, or transcendental, reality of every perception is experienced as unbounded pure consciousness. This may seem very abstract, but while our minds in Unity Consciousness experience everything *in terms* of the unmanifest, infinite Self, we still recognize distinctions between one thing and another. A cat is still a cat and a horse is still a horse; it is just that the different forms do not prevent us from seeing the "oneness of the Self, which is the same in both."[14] According to neuroscientist Tony Nader, this experience of total Unity, infinity, "permeates individual awareness under all conditions of perception, thought, speech, and action."[15]

Bernadette Roberts is an American author and Carmelite nun. Here, she very beautifully explains her experience of Unity Consciousness:

On a bluff above the sea it revealed itself: life is not *in* anything; rather all things are *in* life. The many are immersed in the One, even that which remains when there is no self, this too, is absorbed in the One. No longer a distance between self and the other, all is now known in the immediacy of this identity. Particulars dissolve into the One; individual objects give way to reveal that which is the same throughout all variety and multiplicity.[16]

And this is from a participant in a long peace-creating meditation retreat who appreciates the Self in the ordinary things of life and expresses it in a very natural way:

When walking outside I notice the scenery filled with some new quality, some vitality, beyond description. I see both the unbounded and boundaries existing together, both the tree and the sky as one underlying wholeness, the finite and the infinite blended together in one totality. It is indescribable to be seeing the same scenery in a different way, without having done anything. I see infinity expressed everywhere, and nowhere can I find the finite only.[17]

However unusual each state of consciousness sounds, and however far away from our experience they seem, the reality of higher values of consciousness is never far away. Anyone who has experienced the growth of love or seen colors shine in greater intensity is experiencing something, however little, of refined Cosmic Consciousness. And anyone who has experienced a sense of union with beautiful scenery is experiencing a taste of life in Unity Consciousness. Unity Consciousness is "the supreme awakening of life." Nevertheless, it can refine further to become Brahman Consciousness.

Brahman Consciousness

Brahman is wholeness. It is the wholeness of experience, the ultimate reality, the final stage of Enlightenment. It is a state of *being* the ultimate reality rather than *knowing* ultimate reality on the intellectual level. Brahman is also infinite bliss, unimaginable to the everyday, but completely understood in Brahman Consciousness. As Maharishi Mahesh Yogi writes:

> In the beginning days of Unity only the first focus—the object of first attention—is in terms of the Self, and when this state is lived for a while the object of the second focus also participates in the same value. A little more practice, a little more living of Unity, and even the objects of the third-grade focus and then the fourth-grade focus [are in terms of the Self]. Like that, as we start to live the near environment in terms of the Self, so the ability to appreciate the farther values of the environment in terms of the Self keeps increasing. And the time comes when all the galactic universe, which we can't even see—the whole thing becomes concretely cognized and appreciated in terms of the Self.[18]

Brahman is a reality beyond description, yet somehow, we never stop trying to describe it. Scholars refer to it as *mahantam* (vast, or great), *sarvagata* (omnipresent), or *vibhu* (all-pervading). It is defined as *neti neti*, meaning not this, not this (a way of describing the Ultimate Reality of Brahman by describing what it is not); and s*eti seti*, meaning all features of ultimate reality at the same time (a way of describing the fullness, or *pūrṇa*, aspect of wholeness).

Here, I think I should stop and leave the final description to Maharishi.

> Brahman Consciousness is glorious, it is wholeness, and wholeness with the value of everything. Not that wholeness

that does not incorporate the different values of creation, but every little bit of creation is the expression of its glory. The glory, not in the oneness of wholeness, but the glory of that oneness in wholeness expressed in the multitudes of variety and differences. With such a thing, when the individual unites with Brahman Consciousness, then the joy of life ... I will make you see the joy in this.[19]

On a final note, higher states of consciousness are phases of human development that are universal and natural stages in the unfolding of consciousness. That is why it is good to know about them. Each higher state brings a greater degree of happiness until Brahman Consciousness, which is held to be complete and unshakable joy, dawns. But although there is no published research in reputable journals, is there a way to verify such experiences?

Chapter 14

The Wisdom of the Veda: Verifying Higher States of Consciousness

Ekaṃ sad bahu vadanti.
Truth is one; it is expressed in many ways.

Ṛk Veda[1]

Our knowledge of the world does not come only from Western science; it comes from different sources including the traditional knowledge of humanity and the wisdom of Indigenous people. As far as practical knowledge is concerned, the ancient world had far more knowledge of machines than we think. Mechanical engineering in ancient Greece and China was highly advanced, according to the American Society of Mechanical Engineers. They invented steam engines, clocks, seismometers, screw pumps, and even differential gears. As for mariculture, the cultivation of sea creatures for food, the Indigenous people of British Columbia developed it long before the Europeans settled there.[2] Indeed, the traditional knowledge of humanity has much to offer Western scientists, including knowledge of higher states of consciousness. So, it is to the traditional knowledge of humanity, specifically, the ancient Vedic Literature of India, that we turn now to verify the authenticity of higher states.

The Vedic tradition of knowledge

The word "Vedic" pertains to "Veda" and Veda is a Sanskrit word that means pure or complete knowledge. In the past, the Veda and Vedic Literature have been variously interpreted by scholars as Sanskrit poetry, philosophical dialogue, ritual incantations, philosophical maxims, or translations of the earliest literary record of Indo-Aryan civilization. This is to seriously undervalue the magnitude of the Vedic Literature. The Vedic Literature is an ancient and integrated body of knowledge of reality that expresses and explains the flow of consciousness and the nature of life. To understand this, imagine a house. It begins with a blueprint, an architectural design that contains all the details of the house and gives rise to the building structure. The architectural design of life is held to be the Veda, complete knowledge, and the Vedic Literature is held to be the expression of complete knowledge.

> Veda is like a blueprint of creation, in the sense that it contains every structure and every relationship within it in seed form. The entire creation emerges from Veda, is sustained by Veda, and is administered by Veda. Just as an oak tree seed contains all that there is to know about an oak tree, Veda, as the seed of creation, contains the structure of the material world, along with the principles that underlie every area of knowledge, every discipline, every profession, and indeed every aspect of life.[3]

The Vedic Literature contains many treatises on a vast range of topics, from music to architecture, or from economy to defense. Moreover, every branch of the Vedic Literature is infused with the understanding that consciousness, the Self, gives rise to all things.

The sequence of the Vedic Literature

Maharishi arranged the vast wisdom of the Vedic Literature into the 40 branches shown below, each branch being the flow of pure consciousness and an expression of a specific quality. For instance, Yoga is a Sanskrit word meaning yoke, or union. It expresses the quality of consciousness that unifies all things. The practice of Yoga, however, encourages the ability to unify as it contains techniques such as physical postures (asanas) or breathing techniques (pranayama) that promote emotional health, sleep, and well-being, or happiness.

Ṛk Veda Holistic (Dynamic, Silence) Saṃhitā of Ṛishi, Devatā, and Chhandas		
Ṛishi	**Devatā**	**Chhandas**
Sāma Veda Flowing wakefulness	Yajur Veda Offering and Creating	Atharva Veda Reverberating Wholeness
VEDĀNGA Shikshā Expressing	Kalpa Transforming	Vyākaraṇ Expanding
Jyotish All-Knowing	Chhand Measuring and Quantifying	Nirukta Self-Referral
UPĀNGA Nyāya Distinguishing and Deciding	Vaisheshik Specifying	Sāṃkhya Enumerating
Vedānta Lively Absolute, I-ness or Being	Karma Mīmāṃsā Analyzing	Yoga Unifying
UPA-VEDA Gandharva Veda Integrating and Harmonizing	Dhanur Veda Invincible and Progressive	Sthāpatya Veda Establishing
Kāshyapa Saṃhitā Equivalency	Bhel Saṃhitā Differentiating	Hārīta Saṃhitā Nourishing
Charak Saṃhitā Balancing – Holding Together and Supporting	Sushruta Saṃhitā Separating	Vāgbhatt Saṃhitā Communication and Eloquence
Bhāva Prakāsh Saṃhitā Enlightening	Shārngadhar Saṃhitā Synthesizing	Mādhav Nidān Saṃhitā Diagnosing
BRĀHMAṆA Upanishad Transcending	Āraṇyak Stirring	Brāhmaṇa Structuring
Smṛiti Memory	Purāṇa Ancient and Eternal	Itihāsa Blossoming of Totality
PRĀTISHĀKHYA Ṛk Veda Prātishākhya All-Pervading Wholeness	Shukl-Yajur-Veda Prātishākhya Silencing, Sharing and Spreading	Atharva Veda Prātishākhya Unfolding
Sāma Veda Prātishākhya (Pushpa Sūtram) Unmanifesting the Parts but Manifesting the Whole	Kṛishṇ-Yajur-Veda Prātishākhya Omnipresent	Atharva Veda Prātishākhya (Chaturadhāyī) Dissolving

The 40 aspects of the Veda and Vedic Literature in sequence

The reason for introducing the Veda and Vedic Literature is that while scientific measurements of higher states are as yet in an embryonic stage, verification of higher states of consciousness can be found in the great traditions such as the texts of the Vedic Literature and the *Tao Te Ching*. Some relevant verses of the texts are presented here.

Transcendental Consciousness

If we know the Self, Transcendental Consciousness, then everything else is known. Not knowing Transcendental Consciousness is like seeing light all around without knowing its source in the sun.

Kasminnu bhagavo vigyāte sarvam idaṃ vigyātaṃ bhavatīti
Know that by knowing which everything is known.
(Muṇḍaka Upanishad 1.1.3)

Ekam evādwitīyam
One without a second.
(Chāndogya Upanishad 6.2.1)

Aṇoraṇīyān Mahato–Mahīyān
Smaller than the smallest, larger than the largest.
(Katha Upanishad 1.2.20)

All the many forms of virtue flow from the Tao,
but the nature of the Tao is infinitely illusive.
Illusive, indeed, but at its heart is all being.
Unfathomable, indeed, but at its heart is all spirit,
and spirit is reality.
At its heart is truth. The Tao is eternal and unceasing—
it is present at all beginnings. How do I know this?
By the same Tao.
(*Tao Te Ching*, 21)

This [Self, or Transcendental Consciousness] is a state of inner wakefulness with no object of thought or perception,

just pure consciousness aware of its own unbounded nature. It is wholeness, aware of itself, devoid of differences, beyond the division of subject and object.
(Maharishi Mahesh Yogi)[4]

During [TM] program I slide immediately into Being. It is completely effortless. The experience of silence is completely full. There are no fluctuations and the breath is very still while I float in this infinite field of bliss.
Anonymous[5]

Cosmic Consciousness

The reward of bringing the mind to this state is that the small individual mind grows to the status of the cosmic mind, rising above all its individual shortcomings and limitations.
(Maharishi Mahesh Yogi)[6]

Established in the Self, one overcomes sorrows and suffering.
(Chāndogya Upanishad 7.1.3)

In the field of Cosmic Consciousness, when the mind is brought to the fullest degree of the infusion of absolute Being, by nature the mind functions on the plane of purity in accordance with the natural laws engaged in carrying out the eternal process of evolution...
(Maharishi Mahesh Yogi)[7]

Established in Yoga, O winner of wealth,
perform actions having abandoned attachment
and having become balanced in success and failure,
for balance of mind is called Yoga.
(*Bhagavad Gītā* 2.48.)

(The reference to Yoga here is to the state of Yoga (Transcendental Consciousness), not to the many paths of Yoga.)

The experience of bliss consciousness has become more clear, intense, and stable not only during Transcendental Meditation but also during activity. Now I find that a soft but strong feeling of blissful evenness is present most of the time in both mind and body. Physically it is experienced as an extremely delightful liveliness throughout the body. This evenness is so deep and stable that it is able to maintain its status even in the face of great activity.[8]

Refined Cosmic Consciousness (God Consciousness)

The silent ocean of bliss, the silent ocean of love, begins to rise in waves of devotion. The heart in its state of eternal contentment begins to move.
(Maharishi Mahesh Yogi)[9]

I will give you a parable which may help you understand a little how its form and shape was. It was a round, beautiful, and illuminating light, like the sun, and was of a gold colored red, and this light was so immeasurably beautiful and blissful that I could not compare it with anything else. For if all the stars in the sky were as big and beautiful as the sun, all their splendor could not compare with the beauty my soul had. And it seemed to me that a splendor went out from me that illuminated the whole world, and a blissful day dawned over the whole earth.
(Sophia von Klingnau, 13th or 14th century, Switzerland)[10]

As in a swoon, one instant,
Another sun, ineffable, full-dazzles me,

And all the orbs I knew, with brighter,
unknown orbs, then thousand fold,
One instant of the future land, Heaven's land.
(Walt Whitman)[11]
Everything in my vision is engulfed in a soft golden light
that appears out of thin air, so to speak, and sometimes every
other thing in the visual field, like a chair or curtain or back
of another person's head is embedded in the field of deep
golden light.
Anonymous[12]

Lost in awe at the beauty around me, I must have slipped
into a state of heightened awareness. It is hard—impossible,
really—to put into words the moment of truth that suddenly
came upon me then. Even the mystics are unable to describe
their brief flashes of spiritual ecstasy. It seemed to me, as
I struggled afterward to recall the experience, that self was
utterly absent: I and the chimpanzees, the earth and trees
and air, seemed to merge, to become one with the spirit
power of life itself.
(Jane Goodall)[13]

Unity Consciousness

I am Totality.
(Bṛihadāraṇyaka Upanishad 1.4.2.)

The wise, embracing unity, will become the world's model.
Not striving, they will become enlightened;
not asserting themselves, they will become distinguished;
not boasting, they will be praised;
not building up themselves, they will endure.
As much as they embrace the world, the world will embrace
    them.

Is the old saying, "The broken shall be restored," a false
    hope?
No! All will be restored and return rejoicing.
(Lao Tzu)[14]
He whose self is established in Yoga,
whose vision everywhere is even,
sees the Self in all beings,
and all beings in the Self.
(*Bhagavad Gītā* 6.29)

Only those who attain unity
become what they are meant to be.
(*Tao Te Ching*, 39)

[I]n some peculiar way my consciousness seemed to
have expanded until it was present in a general way,
far beyond even this planet. I was aware of no specific
details of anywhere beyond my immediate vicinity, but I
was a vastness somehow, that in no way contradicted or
conflicted with my limited individuality. Subject and object
had become one—had fused, in some way. There was the
objective world around me, as six months before there had
also been the "simple" vision, but now, as then, there was
a vast "plus." I was both my individual self and in some
greater way, "I" was also everything. Not the personal I,
but the greater I AM. There were no longer two, only one,
I AM.
(Irina Starr)[15]

In activity, I have been feeling a greater intimacy with my
environment than ever before. Everything around me—
people, clouds, grass—feels as dear to me as my Self.
Anonymous[16]

Brahman Consciousness

Contact with Brahm [Brahman] is infinite joy.
(*Bhagavad Gītā* 6.28)

My universe is my Self.
(Taittirīya Upanishad 3.10.)

There is no joy in smallness.
Joy is in the infinite.
(Chāndogya Upanishad 7.23.)

This is the state of Brahman, O Pārtha. Having attained it, a man is not deluded. Established in that, even at the last moment, he attains eternal freedom in divine consciousness. (*Bhagavad Gītā* 2.72.)

Brahma-satyaṃ-jagan mithyā jīvo Brahmaiva nāparaḥ
Brahm is real and the world only appears to be real. This Self, "I," is Totality—Brahman—and none other.
(Shankara)

Higher consciousness, more bliss

We can have experiences of higher states of consciousness at any moment. Experiences could be similar to those included in this chapter, or they could be simple experiences of looking at a sunset and feeling the heart swell with happiness and awe. Either way, they do not necessarily mean we are established in those states. It is more that life gives us reminders along the way to remind us of the real path to complete happiness, the path that some people spend their lives searching for and find in their own backyards.

Pure Transcendental Consciousness is the source of all streams of life and bliss is its fundamental characteristic. It can be experienced, even if for a moment, and is never forgotten.

Out of bliss these beings are born,
In bliss they are sustained,
And to bliss they go and merge again.
(Taittirīya Upanishad 3.6.1.)

However much bliss, or happiness, we experience with Transcendental Meditation practice, the bliss can increase naturally through the addition of a powerful program Maharishi introduced in 1976 called the TM-Sidhi® program. Whereas the mind settles down in an effortless manner with Transcendental Meditation and experiences Transcendental Consciousness, the TM-Sidhi Program cultures our ability to think and act from that level. In so doing, it nourishes the heart, enables thoughts and actions to be fully effective, and is a strong influence on peace creation.

Chapter 15

The Transcendental Meditation-Sidhi Program

To choose doubt as a philosophy of life is akin to choosing immobility as a means of transportation.

Yann Martel[1]

The Transcendental Meditation-Sidhi program, or TM-Sidhi program, is a powerful technology for accelerating the development of consciousness and accompanying bliss. It is also a powerful technology for increasing harmony in society. The mechanics of the TM-Sidhi program are simple:

Specific mental formulas are introduced as gentle impulses of thought during the experience of unbounded awareness. The mind then lets go of this gentle impulse and returns to the state of unbounded awareness. The result is experienced as the specific effect of the particular TM-Sidhi technique.[2]

The TM-Sidhi program is derived from the Yoga Sūtra of Maharishi Patanjali, a great seer of the Vedic tradition of knowledge. The term *Yoga* is usually translated as "union," and the state of Yoga (pure consciousness) signifies that pure consciousness is unified and harmonized with our individual awareness. In other words, the state of Yoga is the state of Cosmic Consciousness. This concept is explained in the first of the *Yoga Sūtra*:

Yogash chitta-vritti-nirodhaḥ
Yoga is the complete settling of the activity of the mind.
Patanjali Yoga Sūtra[3]

Sidhi is another Sanskrit word, defined by Maharishi as "perfection," and *Sūtra* (literally thread) as "aphorisms" or "concise statements," which merge the Self with the finest levels of thinking to accelerate the creation of higher states of consciousness.

The purpose of the program

Experiences reported by many who practice the TM-Sidhi program suggest that the program stabilizes experiences of inner silence gained with Transcendental Meditation practice and unfolds our full potential, thus accelerating growth toward enlightenment. The benefits, including further development of mind-body coordination achieved through practice of Transcendental Meditation, increase with the practice of the TM-Sidhi program as studies have indicated. Moreover, research suggests that TM-Sidhi practitioners experience faster growth toward full development of consciousness than would normally be the case. Many practitioners report increasing inner silence, fulfillment, and an expanded ability to maintain inner silence even while taking part in strenuous activity. Nevertheless, the most often reported benefit of the TM-Sidhi program is the experience of increasing levels of bliss, as this next quote demonstrates:

During the TM-Sidhi program my awareness was in pure consciousness. I kept experiencing indescribable bliss, an indescribable ecstatic feeling that I felt could not be contained within myself.[4]

Increased happiness can be experienced while resting *after* the TM-Sidhi program too as this meditator reveals.

After [the TM-Sidhi] program, my field of perception was pervaded by a sort of quiet bliss—a soft, understated, but

115

thorough happiness—born of an abiding sense of deep and utter wholeness, the felt presence of my own indivisible Being, holding all experience within it.[5]

The most powerful sutra of the TM-Sidhi techniques comes in 3.42 of Maharishi Patañjali's *Yoga Sūtra* and refers to movement through space. While this movement is referred to as Yogic Flying, it is experienced as hopping. Researcher Dr. Fred Travis notes that:

The EEG pattern in the hopping stage does not seem to be a muscle artifact of body movements for several reasons: 1) there is very little power in the theta and beta frequencies; 2) there is no visually apparent muscle activity in the EEG; and 3) the controls who jumped rather than practiced Yogic Flying did not show this pattern. The Yogic Flying EEG pattern does not seem to be generated by the motor system sending signals to the muscle system, which suggests that the Yogic Flying program is more than just the physical act of jumping. In follow-up research, the main difference between the two groups, as measured by EEG, appeared in the two seconds before the body rose in the air when practitioners of the Yogic Flying technique reported experiencing extreme bliss and exhilaration.[6]

EEG studies have demonstrated that when the body moves forward during Yogic Flying, mind and body are completely integrated. It is the practice of this Yoga Sūtra that has the maximum effect on peace creation as will be seen in the following chapters.

Thus, this book now moves away from the path of creating a happy world through creating happy individuals and moves toward the path to creating a happy world through societal, or collective, well-being. The reason it is even possible to talk

116

about this rests on the evidence of more than 50 demonstrations and more than 20 peer-reviewed studies indicating that the Transcendental Meditation and TM-Sidhi programs, when practiced in large groups, can counteract intense national and international stress, and reduce conflict. The peer-review process is still a reliable way to gauge the worth of an academic paper, and papers on the Maharishi Effect are subject to far more scrutiny than the usual two or three reviewers. It is sometimes useful to be beyond the norm.

Looking forward

Many societies today have problems of divisions and intolerance, but there seems to be more unity in the idea that social divisions are dangerous than there is in finding a reasonable solution to divisiveness. In the end, it comes down to finding something deeper than intellectual arguments, which try to solve conflict on the level of the conflict. As Maharishi brings to light, it is the experience of Transcendental Consciousness that increases tolerance in human behavior. The experience "leaves both parties in added joyfulness, energy, love and harmony, while at the same time it creates an influence of peace, harmony, joyfulness and freshness in the atmosphere."[7]

Nowadays, the importance of joy, or happiness, is understood, otherwise there would not be a World Happiness Report. Happiness matters, and to look for happiness outside is generally not as powerful as looking for happiness inside. But happiness is based on peace. Therefore, to create a happy world, a peaceful world must first be created, and there are many good organizations dedicated to achieving this goal. The problem is that we are in the 21st century, and peace is still elusive. Maybe it is time to create peace through other, less conventional means, and time to look deeper than the level of the problem if we truly desire a peaceful, happy world.

Part III

Peace, the Basis of Happiness

Chapter 16

Questions

When I came back from Afghanistan, I was angry, depressed, and suicidal. Transcendental Meditation has lifted my depression, eased my pain and given me my life back.

Luke Jensen, a veteran of Operation Enduring Freedom[1]

In the 15th century BCE, a battle took place between the Egyptian army under Thutmose III,[2] a young pharaoh who had never before seen battle, and the Canaanite army under Durusha. Durusha was king of Kadesh and now barely remembered in the West, and Kadesh was a region in what is now western Syria. At the time of Durusha, the Egyptian empire controlled most of Canaan and Syria, but a revolt was about to take place. The defiant Canaanite army, consisting of around 150 rebellious princes, all of whom had struggled under the Egyptian yoke for too long, marched to Megiddo, an ancient town overlooking the plain of Esdraelon, to await the Egyptian army. The siege of Megiddo by the Egyptians lasted for many months, but the inhabitants of Megiddo could not hold out forever and the city surrendered. After the surrender, the young pharaoh spared Megiddo and its citizens but took home the spoils.

There were battles before this one, but the battle of Megiddo is famous because it was the first one to have a relatively dependable record of its progress, carved into the walls of Karnak, the site of the Temple of Amun in ancient Thebes, Egypt. Interestingly, the battle of Megiddo, or at least the name, is believed by some scholars to be the origin of the Hebrew word Armageddon—Har-Magedon, meaning Mount of Megiddo.

The battle of Megiddo may have been the first war recorded, but it was not the last. The endless stream of conflicts over three and a half thousand years has seemed relentless. Egyptian wars, Roman wars, Byzantine wars, Crusades, European wars: the list goes on and on. As *Creating a Happy World* is being written, a war between Russia and Ukraine is raging that could threaten peace in Europe and the wider world.

At the time of Thutmose III, the Egyptians were fighting a very real threat from rebellious warlords gathering in the north who were determined to remove themselves from Egyptian control and crush Egypt itself at a vulnerable moment. In our time, the Russian/Ukraine conflict hinges on two primary issues: the expansion of the North Atlantic Treaty Organization (NATO), perceived as a threat to Russian security, and Russian president Vladimir Putin's conviction that Russia, Belarus, and the Ukraine should "share a political destiny both today and in the future."[3] As reported by Reuters, on February 21, 2022, Vladimir Putin stated:

Russia assumed obligations to repay the entire Soviet debt in return for the newly independent states giving up part of their foreign assets. In 1994, such agreements were reached with Ukraine, but they were not ratified by Ukraine ... (Ukraine) preferred to act in such a way that in relations with Russia they had all the rights and advantages, but did not bear any obligations ... From the very first steps they began to build their statehood on the denial of everything that unites us. They tried to distort the consciousness, the historical memory of millions of people, entire generations living in Ukraine.[4]

The right of leaders to conquer other nations was traditionally accepted in the past, but the Russian/Ukrainian war is a betrayal of our belief that the human race has matured. Moreover, the current conflict is a war conducted by the Russian government with the aim of taking away the very identity of the Ukrainian people. To quote the Prussian general, Carl von Clausewitz (1780–1831), "War is a mere continuation of policy by other means."[5] Other means, in the case of Russia and Ukraine, are the extreme methods of the Russian leadership to enforce unwelcome policies on the Ukrainians.

Wars are not generated by peaceful people; they are generated by those who are not at peace and therefore are not happy. As the *Bhagavad Gītā* states, "For one without peace how can there be happiness?"[6] But peace can be tenuous because conflicts are not limited to war. Conflicts, whether local or national, can be violent and while wars may slowly be in retreat, the world is still riddled with violence committed by aggressive people. Mass shootings in the U.S. Sandy Hook. Buffalo. Texas. These are some of the latest instances of appalling violence that are not created by peaceful minds. And the organizations that aim to create a more peaceful world do not appear to be looking in the right place for the root cause of violence and the root cause of unhappiness in a nation.

We cannot do anything about violence on either the individual or the global scale if we do not know the root cause of it because the underlying problems of violence are bound up with who we are and how determined we are to create lasting happiness for every nation. NASA can send a mission to Mars, but scientists are still arguing about the one thing that is fundamental to human knowledge, and that is consciousness, the "mysterious" thing that, as we will see, is profoundly linked to the possibility of peace and resulting civil happiness. Organizations such as the United Nations, the King Center for Nonviolent Social Change, the M.K. Gandhi Institute, and the Desmond Tutu Peace Foundation, the very organizations we look to for solutions, are not inclined at present to strongly encourage practices that promote enlightenment. But since, according to the *Bhagavad Gītā*, peace is the basis of happiness, fostering happiness through growing enlightenment seems to be the best way to achieve peace and happiness, and happiness is important for everyone.

The Dalai Lama holds that the purpose of life is to find happiness.[7] The *Bhagavad Gītā* states: "For one without peace, how can there be happiness?" The Vietnamese Buddhist monk Thich Nhat Hanh says, "When you are excited you are not peaceful. True happiness is based on peace."[8] And Maharishi Mahesh Yogi maintains that "Absolute bliss being always there, the experience of happiness thus depends upon the degree of steadiness of the mind. If the mind is more collected, more peaceful, it experiences more happiness."[9] The idea that happiness is based on peace is crucial to creating a happy world. Without peace, how can there be happiness?

Reason for despair or inspiration to delve deeper?

For millennia, human beings have fought each other and destroyed the beauty and learning of great cities. People who ought to have lived until a quiet old age have been struck down in battle, and the menace of international or domestic terrorism is still striking unexpectedly. Consider the 2013 bombing during the 117th running of the Boston Marathon.

On April 15, 2013, Patriots' Day, the very day that two centuries earlier had begun America's Revolutionary War, three spectators were killed, and 260 others were wounded when two bombs exploded near the finish line. A fierce hunt resulted in the capture of one of the bombers, 19-year-old Dzhokhar Tsarnaev, who had been born in the former Soviet republic of Kyrgyzstan. Together with his older brother, 26-year-old Tamerlan Tsarnaev, the pair planned and carried out the bombing. The reason for the bombing, according to a note found in the boat where the 19-year-old was hiding, was retaliation for U.S. wars conducted in Muslim countries.[10]

Such horrific events can make people feel helpless. No one expects an attack like this at what should be a happy day of celebration. To search for answers, it is not enough to analyze the minds of terrorists or the minds of national and international leaders. Research indicates that the answer to war and violence does not come from that level. So, what can ordinary people do to prevent wars and all the unwanted misery that accompanies them? The conventional options are limited.

- Never glorify war
- Try to understand both sides of an international argument
- Support the creation of international criminal courts that can bring perpetrators of war crimes to justice.

But it seems that these solutions are not enough because the causes of conflict run deep, and therefore we have to look deeper. There is evidence to suggest that unrest and violence, and by inference, lack of peace and happiness, are the result of a lack of order in collective consciousness, the interconnectedness of all the individual consciousnesses that make up a group or a nation. There is also evidence to suggest that the Transcendental Meditation technique is not only beneficial for our minds, bodies, and emotional well-being, but can have a positive impact on collective consciousness. But is this influence real, and if it is real, is it correlation or causation?

Chapter 17

Collective Consciousness

All occurrences of violence, negativity, conflict, crises, or problems in any society "are just the expression of growth of stress in collective consciousness. When the level of stress becomes sufficiently great, it bursts out into large-scale violence, war, and civil uprising necessitating military action."

Maharishi Mahesh Yogi[1]

Maharishi's statement above is echoed by the film director and philanthropist David Lynch, who said, "The problem of violence, at its source, is stress—the escalating buildup of political and societal stress in collective consciousness that fuels conflict and warfare ... The only solution is to reduce the stress in collective consciousness—in society as a whole. Truly, there is no other way."[2] If the causes of conflict and violence lie in collective consciousness, then collective consciousness must be better understood.

Durkheim's collective consciousness

The French sociologist Émile Durkheim coined the term *collective consciousness*, or *conscience collective*. Durkheim described it in this way: "The totality of beliefs and sentiments common to average citizens of the same society forms a determinate system which has its own life; one may call it the collective or common conscience."[3] He referred to collective consciousness as: a) being independent of the particular conditions in which the individuals are placed; and b) having properties, conditions of existence, and modes of development that are similar to those of individuals. Durkheim also concluded, "In the large, happiness coincides with a healthy state,"[4] which makes sense from the perspective that if the state is healthy, then it must be because the individuals who make up that state are healthy.[5]

Durkheim's understanding of a *conscience collective* evolved into the modern understanding of collective consciousness as the shared beliefs, attitudes, and ideas that are a unifying force within a group, be it the military, society, or nation, or even the whole world. It is a cliché to say that the way we see the world depends on the emotional lens through which we view it, but it is true. Our world, our society, is as we are. To change society, we must change ourselves because what we are produces the type of society we live in, the type of media that is prevalent, the political system, and even the type of medicine that is favored. The reason for this is that we pour our thoughts, feelings, and sentiments into a collective mix, a local or national collective consciousness that generates the way we live and the way that scientific discoveries, artistic expressions, and general ideas are interpreted and accepted. To quote Maharishi, collective consciousness is "the essence of a nation that continues generation after generation."[6]

Levels within levels

There are many levels to collective consciousness, individual consciousness, family consciousness, city consciousness, national consciousness, and world consciousness. We can understand the interconnection of these as Russian nesting (*matryoshka*) dolls, each one placed inside the other in ever decreasing sizes. Every level influences the other levels and in turn is influenced by them. If the influence is positive, then harmony results. If the influence is negative, then disharmony will push its way through. At the basis of all levels is Transcendental Consciousness.

For Maharishi Mahesh Yogi, experiences of Transcendental Consciousness, the unity at the source of all life's rich diversity, are the basis of a harmonious, happy, and tolerant society. The experience of Transcendental Consciousness is, therefore, the only reliable way in the long-term to harmonize each level of collective consciousness. This can be explained with reference to the human body.

In the same way that a human being is made of trillions of cells, all of which contribute to the organs and tissues that make up the human body, society is made up of its own cells, the people who live in it, help to run it, and retire in it. Each individual may not describe themselves as a cell in the body of society, they may not even be aware of the reasons why they act as they do, but they are contributing to collective consciousness all the same. That is why some towns have a tense feel about them and others have a harmonious and relaxed feel. It is collective consciousness that determines whether society is unified, peaceful, and happy, or whether society is divided and disorderly, with continuous infighting, everyone afraid to say what they think and feel, and everyone afraid to deviate from the norm in creative pursuits. This does not produce a happy, united society at peace with itself and at peace with the rest of the world.

If collective consciousness is a reality, it must be valid in every sphere of life, including the arts.

Collective consciousness within the arts?

Throughout time, artistic styles arise which reflect the character of the age. They reach a point of development and then are overtaken by new styles. There is not much peer-reviewed scientific analysis of this process, but a good case can be made for suggesting that artistic trends reflect the nature of the people and therefore the nature of collective consciousness. Art is created by people, and everything we create is a reflection of who we are. An artist's work is an extension of the artist and an artist in any genre cannot help but reflect the ethos of the time, its cultural spirit appearing in the ideas and beliefs of the people. Alan Rich, former chief music critic of the *New York Herald Tribune* and contributing editor of *New York* magazine, points out that the separate arts do not exist in isolation.

> Together they provide a key to the prevailing creative impulses of their time; a firsthand report, worded directly from the inner consciousness of the creators themselves. Together they form a body which draws upon the spirit of the time, each in its own way.[7]

Artists, whether painters, sculptors, musicians, or writers, refer back to their inner perceptions and experiences, but they also refer back to the experiences of the time, the subtle changes in collective consciousness. As noted above, scientific research on this subject is somewhat lacking, but a measure of support comes from Alex Edmans and his colleagues in their 2022 paper, "Music Sentiment and Stock Returns Around the World."

The authors suggest that the positivity of songs that we choose to listen to is "positively correlated with same-week equity market returns and negatively correlated with next-week returns, consistent with sentiment-induced temporary mispricing."[8] Apparently, the music we listen to is also a predictor of increases in net mutual fund flows. Not only that, but "absolute sentiment precedes a rise in stock market volatility."

Can this be coincidence? It is pioneering research certainly, but is also an indication that the national mood influences the stock market. Similarly, musical trends in different periods cannot be written off as intellectual ideas spreading among different people; they seem to arise at the same time in different artistic genres. Moreover, if an artist, musician, or writer is considered "ahead of their time," it is, according to this view, because the sensitive antennae of the artist or musician is unconsciously aware of changes in collective consciousness.

If we consider other research, particularly that published in the *Journal of Consciousness Studies*, one study authored by Allan Combs and Stanley Krippner is relevant to this book. Combs and Krippner discuss supportive neurological and social evidence for the idea of collective consciousness.[9] Referring to spiritual traditions and oral cultures such as the Australian Aborigines, Combs and Krippner suggest that some kind of entanglement in the activity of human brains may be involved.

Entangled dancing

Entanglement is the term used by scientists for an emergent property that is seen at vastly small subatomic scales. Entanglement arises when two particles, such as a pair of photons or electrons, become entangled and remain entangled (connected) even when separated by immense distances. In fact, the exquisite dance of the entangled particles emerges not from one of the particles, but from the connections between them. If researchers measure the "spin" of each of the entangled particles, they will find that the pair are infinitely correlated. If the spin of one particle is "up" then the spin of the other particle will be "down." Or both will be up or both will be down. Whatever way around, there is always correlation between them. Scientists may argue about the entanglement phenomenon, but it is real and there is nothing strange or "spooky" about it. Entanglement does not just occur between two particles. Apparently, it can occur among millions, even billions of particles, in fact, throughout the atoms of living creatures and even metals.[10] As the authors of "Collective Consciousness and the Social Brain" state:

All this brings us back full circle to the idea that at a subtle level of connectivity the brains of individuals who share the ordinary collective consciousness of intimate social groupings might, given optimal circumstances, also experience strong collective consciousness supported by the neuronal processes of their separate nervous systems that fall into a simpatico or resonance, like the ticking of clocks on the same wall. This would be equivalent to a kind of entanglement of activity in individual brains and offers a possible solution to the binding problem of human collective consciousness.[11]

While this quote does not suggest that collective consciousness exists on many levels, it does point out that any group forms a collective personality, or a collective consciousness, whether the members of the group are aware of it or not. With entanglement, the important thing to remember is that observing one of the particles can immediately give information about the other entangled particles irrespective of the distance between them. Even more importantly, any action occurring in one of them will immediately impact the other entangled particles, and when many particles become entangled, they act as a unified whole.

All for one and one for all

The military is not immune to the influence of collective consciousness. As the 5th century Chinese military commander Sun Tzu wrote in *The Art of War*, "He will win whose army is animated by the same spirit throughout all its ranks."[12] Here, Sun Tzu is clearly referring to the importance of unity in an army. Sun Tzu also emphasizes the importance of inspiring the army with unity of purpose.[13] However, first and foremost, he believes that "supreme excellence consists in breaking the enemy's resistance without fighting."[14] For Sun Tzu, "the highest form of generalship is to balk the enemy's plans; the next best is to prevent the junction of the enemy's forces; the next in order is to attack the enemy's army in the field."[15] As a military commander, he does not appear to rate fighting as highly as avoiding fighting, but avoiding fighting is easier said than done, judging by the large number of wars that have taken place since his time.

So how can we create a peaceful, happy nation, even a peaceful, happy world? When treaties last, and many do, then nations can sleep easily. Unfortunately, treaties can be unreliable in which case no one sleeps easily.

Insecure treaties

The 1972 Biological Weapons Convention, a treaty that bans the production and use of biological and toxin weapons, was widely welcomed. Signatories of the treaty guaranteed never to develop, produce, stockpile, or otherwise acquire or retain:

- microbial or other biological agents, or toxins whatever their origin or method of production, of types and in quantities that have no justification for prophylactic, protective or other peaceful purposes
- weapons, equipment or means of delivery designed to use such agents or toxins for hostile purposes or in armed conflict.[16]

But even as the treaty was being signed, the Soviet Union was already planning a biological weapons research, development, and production program on a huge scale. By 2018, many governments, including those of the governments of the U.K., Canada, Israel, Germany, U.S., France, and Russia, were known to carry out covert research into bioweaponry. The problem is that when one country begins research into biological weaponry, other countries feel they have to compete. The threat of bioweapons is also not the sole province of governments. The Japanese terrorist group Aum Shinrikyo carried out a deadly attack using sarin (a chemical nerve agent) attack on a Tokyo subway in 1987.

Even the 1968 Nuclear Non-Proliferation Treaty, which obligates nations to regulate the safe use of nuclear energy, prevent the spreading of nuclear weapons, and work toward nuclear disarmament, cannot be held to be completely reliable. By 2006, there had already been violations of the treaty involving Iraq, Iran, Libya, and North Korea, hardly friends of the U.S. and its allies. Then again, in 2019, the U.S. and Russia pulled out of the Intermediate-Range Nuclear Forces Treaty, designed to ban missiles with ranges between 310 and 3,400 miles. At the time of writing, the president of the Russian Federation, Vladimir Putin, is threatening nuclear war. So much for disarmament. So much for the reliability of major treaties.

Given the reality of the world we live in, what more can we do to create a peaceful planet, bearing in mind that peace is the basis for happiness? As Sherlock Holmes said in *The Sign of the Four*, "Eliminate all other factors, and the one which remains must be the truth."[17] The truth, in this case, appears to be the Maharishi Effect.

Chapter 18

The Maharishi Effect

If the world is a subject for rational thought it is all of one piece; the same laws are found everywhere, and everything is connected with everything else; and if this is so, there is nothing mean, and nothing in which may not be seen the universal law.

Oliver Wendell Holmes Jr.[1]

If consciousness is all there is, then everything is connected. While it may seem difficult to reconcile this with everyday perception of the world, it becomes a lived experience in higher states of consciousness, and can be upheld by recent research on collective consciousness. When the mind goes beyond every tiny thought and feeling and experiences deep peace, then the mind has expanded to the infinite level of the omnipresent Self, Transcendental Consciousness. In this very desirable state, higher brain wave coherence is generated, thus making us more coherent, peaceful, and capable of more orderly thinking and behavior. By higher brain wave coherence, we mean that the different waves of the brain, alpha, beta, theta, gamma, are moving synchronously with each other. When this occurs in groups practicing the Transcendental Meditation and TM-Sidhi program, increased coherence radiates out into the collective consciousness. This is known as the Maharishi Effect and results in a boost of orderly thinking in the population as a whole, which can soften the atmosphere and, according to the evidence, decrease crime and conflict.

The Maharishi Effect

The Maharishi Effect was named after Maharishi Mahesh Yogi who first predicted that Transcendental Meditation practice could influence the collective consciousness of society in a positive direction. As early as 1962, Maharishi stated:

> The day one-tenth of the adult population of the world begins to meditate a half-hour morning and evening and begins to emit an influence of peace and harmony from the deepest level of consciousness—from that day, the atmosphere of the world, this negative atmosphere of the world, will be neutralized, and from that day will dawn the chance of no war for centuries to come.[2]

Elsewhere, Maharishi is reported as saying that "while 10% would be ideal, even if only 1% of the world's population meditated it would be sufficient to do away with the hatred that causes war."[3] There is a very simple reason why Transcendental Meditation has this effect, and it lies in our understanding of Transcendental Consciousness. Again, Maharishi states:

> Because consciousness is the basis of all that is there—here, there, and everywhere—it is the quantum level of life, the very basic level of life. If the attention reaches that level, what happens is like the small pebble falling on the silent bed of the water. A small pebble falls, creating impulses. These impulses reach all the far places and all the water. Just like that, when the conscious mind of one single individual transcends, we can imagine the thrills being created on that silent level of consciousness which is the omnipresent reality. This pulsating consciousness of the individual creates impulses of life all over, and because this is the very fundamental level of life of everyone, everyone's thinking, everyone's consciousness is influenced by that ... The whole society becomes more positive in its trends, more positive in its thinking. The awareness of the whole population is

influenced tremendously. That is why the criminals change, negativity changes. A man thinking like that today, he thinks in a different way tomorrow.[4]

In the above passage, Maharishi brings to light that even 1% of a population practicing Transcendental Meditation will create a positive influence on the quality of life for the population. And with the TM-Sidhi program, the benefits received from Transcendental Meditation practice alone are accelerated. Over the years, evidence has accumulated to show that only the square root of 1% of the population practicing the TM and TM-Sidhi program is needed to create more harmonious trends in the population.[5] Of course, these figures are merely guidelines. Sometimes, a stressed city may need more than the normal 1% to effect a change. One can also ask whether it is the ardent wishes of meditators for peace that creates the effect, or something deeper. Once more, the answer lies in the experience of Transcendental Consciousness.

Transcendental Consciousness is the basis of individual consciousness, and individual consciousness is the basis of collective consciousness. Thus, experiences of Transcendental Consciousness by large numbers of people are central to the Maharishi Effect as they enliven the deep, inner silence of Transcendental Consciousness throughout the field of consciousness.[6] The Maharishi Effect itself is upheld by more than 50 demonstrations and over 20 peer-reviewed studies stretching from 1974 to 2022, all of which suggest that improving collective consciousness through large groups practicing Transcendental Meditation and the TM-Sidhi program can result in improvements in the quality of life in society without the use of force.

The history of the 1% and the square root of 1% effect was explained in *An Antidote to Violence: Evaluating the Evidence* (co-authored by me). Rather than repeat what has already been documented there, I am only going to present a few specific locations where the Maharishi Effect has created a difference, beginning with a global operation called the World Peace Project.

The World Peace Project

The World Peace Project was inspired by an appeal for help from several Nicaraguan citizens caught in the middle of a revolution in their country. The appeal generated an immediate response from Maharishi and the Transcendental Meditation Organization. For ten weeks in the Fall of 1978, groups of Transcendental Meditation teachers traveled to some of the world's worst trouble spots, including Nicaragua, to quietly practice the TM-Sidhi program together in hotels, motels, and meeting rooms. The list of countries also included Guatemala, Iran, Zimbabwe (formerly Rhodesia), and Zambia. The World Peace Project participants did not interact with the local population or tour the countryside. Instead, they practiced the TM-Sidhi program from within the confines of their hotels and meeting rooms, spreading an influence of peace into the national collective consciousness, and bringing calm to the people. During this time, changes in each country were measured through an independent data source, the Conflict and Peace Data Bank (COPDAB), the largest data bank in the world that documented conflict in international affairs on a daily basis.

Lead researcher David Orme-Johnson "compared the data for the length of time each group was present in a specific country with a comparison period of the same length in the months immediately before the peace-creating group arrived."[7] He noted a difference between the months before the TM-Sidhi practitioners arrived and the months afterward. Hostile events decreased, verbal hostilities reduced, and cooperation between conflicting parties increased. While stories can be told about many of the trouble spots, here, two TM-Sidhi practitioners give their firsthand experiences of the situation in Iran and Guatemala.

Notes from Iran

At the end of 1978, Iran was in turmoil and a revolution seemed more than likely as many people were unhappy with the existing regime (headed by the Shah of Iran) and wanted to see major changes in the governance of the country.

As part of an overall "Peace Project," which was aimed at researching the impact of sending groups of yogic flyers to quell violence in "trouble spots," I traveled from London to Tehran with a sizeable group of other TM-Sidhi practitioners from the U.K. Maharishi European Research University, which was managing the project, had earlier sent a larger group from the United States there, but this had been insufficient in number to dampen the turmoil. As such, the BBC, along with several other media groups, were predicting that a demonstration planned for the following weekend would erupt into terrible violence.

Soon after arriving it was decided that our group should practice our yogic flying in a separate hotel from the U.S. group so that the route of the demonstration would be directly between the two hotels. It was hoped that this, together with the increased numbers of yogic flyers, would generate sufficient coherence to ensure that the demonstration proceeded in an orderly and peaceful way.

We were heartened by the time the demonstration began as the violence around the country already seemed to be reduced, which we put down to the increased numbers of yogic flyers. Nevertheless, I found it personally a little worrying, as did others, as we had not experienced such a situation before. My worries proved unfounded, however, as, much to everyone's astonishment, despite hundreds of thousands of people joining the march it all went off with virtually no violence, a fact that was reported upon with surprise by most of the international media.

In the days that followed the demonstration the turmoil settled down and we were all feeling increasingly confident that we would be able to establish a peaceful situation in Tehran. It was our hope to soon teach a permanent group of practicing yogic flyers made up of Iranian people that would maintain peace and coherence on a permanent basis. This wasn't to be, however, as the visas for the American group came to an end 1–2 weeks later, and finding it impossible to extend them, they were forced to leave the country. The effect was exactly what we had witnessed when our group arrived in Tehran, *but this time in reverse!* Violence was increasingly reported across the country; machine guns were regularly going off in Tehran's city center (including close to our hotel) and the media were predicting an ever-worsening situation from the standpoint of violence. We were unable to bring in reinforcements of yogic flyers and as the violence continued daily, we found ourselves having to stay within the confines of our hotel for days on end, as per the advice of the British Embassy. Eventually, our visas were to expire too, so it was with a heavy heart that we all left Iran. Shortly afterward, we read how serious violence had erupted across the country. The Shah was then forced to leave the country and the Islamic Republic of Iran (that still rules today) was established.

Looking back, I realize that our group of yogic flyers experienced one of the most concrete demonstrations of the Maharishi Effect one could possibly imagine. We witnessed firsthand an almost immediate quelling of violence upon our arrival and an increase in violence just as soon as the U.S. group was forced to leave. This was followed by an explosion of violence once both groups had left.

R.H.[8]

Notes from Guatemala

From Oct. 14 to Nov. 12, 1978, we regularly did group practice of the TM and TM-Sidhi program all morning and in the evening. Our only recreation was to go to the terrace on top of the hotel and enjoy the beautiful view of the city. Every day from the top of the building, I looked down at the telephone building across the street. In the first days after we arrived, I saw that the soldiers guarding the building were very tense. They were nervous. Everyone was a threat. They always held their guns ready to shoot. The soldiers would point their weapons and challenge anyone who came near the telephone building, even the people who worked there.

After a few days, the soldiers became progressively more relaxed. Instead of holding their guns ready to shoot, their rifles were hanging across their backs. They calmly talked with the people who passed by or entered the building. As the days passed, the soldiers were laughing and joking with each other and people who entered the building. It was an amazing transformation to watch. The soldiers went from a very tense mindset to a very peaceful and even happy one. In the third week of our stay, a major protest was scheduled that would involve thousands of people on the streets of downtown Guatemala near us. People were angry about the shooting of several students. Violence was expected. However, instead of violence, the huge demonstration was very peaceful. The government officials and most citizens were shocked. They thought for certain there would be fighting and blood in the streets. Instead, they got peace.

R.H.[9]

Iran and Guatemala are examples of what can happen when a large enough group of TM-Sidhi practitioners get together to bring peace to a country locked in turmoil. Another example is Mozambique, but what happened in Mozambique is far more extraordinary.

Chapter 19

Peace in a Time of National Heartbreak

Peace comes from being able to contribute the best that we have, and all that we are, toward creating a world that supports everyone. But it is also securing the space for others to contribute the best that they have and all that they are.

Hafsat Abiola[1]

The Mozambique experiment began in the Republic of Zambia, home to human cultures going back 300,000 years. Around 60 Transcendental Meditation instructors traveled from New York to the capital of Zambia, Lusaka, in the late summer of 1978. All 60 were practitioners of the Transcendental Meditation and TM-Sidhi program, and all were aware they were part of a global initiative to calm down the world's most troubled areas. Many of their friends and colleagues were going to a variety of hotspots including Nicaragua and Iran, as described in the previous chapter, but they were going to Zambia.

The group arrived in Lusaka after a long flight from New York and moved into a motel. During the first night, they were kept awake by the sound of automatic gunfire from the nearby jungle, but only on the first night. From then on, they stayed in the motel for two months and did not mix with the local population. Every day, they began their group practice in the morning and continued with it until lunch, and then started again in the afternoon. Once they began their meditation program, they never heard the gunfire again. All they felt was the bliss of the practice and a sense of humility that they were able to help a country that had suffered from civil war for such a dismally long time. This is what one participant had to say when their two months in Zambia came to an end:

Our last night was a dinner with President Kenneth Kaunda and his family and the Secretary of State and his family. Here was the head of state, a beautiful African man wearing the traditional, colorful robes, crying in front of our entire group because we had to leave. And it was a real letdown when the BBC reported the violence flared up five days later. That was the saddest moment of all.

M.H.[2]

According to reports, President Kaunda had wanted to start a permanent group of Transcendental Meditation and TM-Sidhi practitioners in Zambia but was not able to do so. Instead, he contacted President Chissano of Mozambique, a country that had also suffered a long and brutal civil war. President Chissano not only listened as President Kaunda told him the results of the World Peace Project in Zambia, but also acted on this information.

Mozambique

Mozambique's civil war began in 1977 and ended in 1992. During those years, Mozambique was a frightening and violent mess. FRELIMO, Frente de Libertação de Moçambique (Mozambique Liberation Front), a Marxist group, was fighting the South African- and Rhodesian-backed rebel militias known as RENAMO, Resistência Nacional Moçambicana (Mozambican National Resistance). Although this might have seemed like a local quarrel, it was in fact a proxy war fought between the US, which supported the rebels, and the former Soviet Union, which supported the government forces. Estimations indicate that one million people died as a result of the conflict or famine, out of a total population of only fourteen million.[3] Following such a vicious conflict, the Mozambique government, subsequently headed by Joaquim Chissano, signed a highly fragile peace agreement with RENAMO in Rome in 1992, and UN peacekeepers moved into Mozambique.

There is little doubt that the presence of a peacekeeping military helped the country through the transition from violence to a peace that seemed almost unobtainable. Nevertheless, in the minds of President Joaquim Chissano and his generals, another event helped to soften the atmosphere, and made the apparently unobtainable peace ... obtainable. President Chissano took the advice of Kenneth Kaunda, agreed to learn the Transcendental Meditation technique, and never looked back. "First," he said, "I started the practice of TM (Transcendental Meditation) myself, then introduced the practice to my close family, then to my cabinet of ministers, then to my government officers, and then to the military. The result has been political peace and balance in nature."[4]

On the orders of President Chissano, all military and police recruits were instructed to practice Transcendental Meditation for 20 minutes twice a day, and somewhere in excess of 16,000 soldiers learned Transcendental Meditation and its advanced program, the TM-Sidhi program.[5] To add to this, around 30,000 civilians also learned Transcendental Meditation and a further 3,000 started the TM-Sidhi program. The effect was striking. Mozambique's economic growth rose to 19%, and crime levels decreased. According to the former Mozambique defense minister Tobias Dai, "The implementation of the Transcendental Meditation and TM-Sidhi programs ... to the Armed Forces of Mozambique was worth the effort and the results were in line with what was predicted."[6] The tragedy was that with the demobilization of troops, practice of the peace-creating programs stopped, and the previous tendencies of higher collective stress, as determined by crime indices and tension in the country, crept back.

A president to remember

Joaquim Chissano is known as a quiet man with extraordinary negotiating skills. At a state banquet in Maputo, the nation's capital, on November 16, 1999, the U.K.'s late Queen, Elizabeth II, praised Mozambique's journey from civil war to peace. Here is part of her speech.

The recognition by all parties that it was only through peace that there could be any prospect for resolving differences, and Mozambique's commitment to reconciliation and democracy, offer a valuable lesson to countries in Africa and elsewhere still riven by conflict ... Mozambique is now one of Africa's success stories. It has been able to emerge from the fires of internal conflict through solidarity with its neighbours, with other states across this great continent of Africa, and with its newfound Commonwealth friends around the world.[7]

When President Chissano came to power, Mozambique was in a state of economic collapse and its people were in despair. When he left power, the nation was stable and entering the world family. Hence, in recognition of his achievements, President Chissano was awarded the first Mo Ibrahim Prize for African leadership in October 2007 by Kofi Annan, the former secretary-general of the United Nations. Annan stated as he awarded the prize, "President Chissano's achievements in bringing peace, reconciliation, stable democracy, and economic progress to his country greatly impressed the committee. So, too, did his decision to step down without seeking the third term the constitution allowed."[8]

President Chissano continued to play a role in furthering peace and stability in Mozambique, in the African Union, and in the UN, and his work has singled him out as a great leader capable of bringing about peace, stability, and economic progress in the aftermath of civil war. In 2010, he gave this message to the Washington D.C. Gotabgaa Conference, a registered nonprofit organization that focuses on connecting, uplifting, and empowering individuals and families through community programs:

I have been given the privilege of helping in some way to restore peace and unity in your country (Kenya) during the conflict which was generated after the last elections and (am) pleased that all efforts have been made inside the country and outside the country to promote this peace.

I know that we can search for peace looking into the unity of each other, but this cannot be effective—cannot be effective—while we don't have a peace each one in himself. We have to have our internal peace first. We have to know deeply what we are. And there are many ways of knowing oneself. We know the societies, the history of each society, and so on. But (for) one to know himself, he must be living in a deep knowledge of his inside. There are many ways of looking for where we're coming from and where we're going to. But to know ourselves we can reach when we practice a meditation which brings a silence for some time every day, so that we be ourselves out of the tensions we create every day.

We live in tensions, we live in stress, and so we cannot find ourselves. We are preoccupied with external things which surround us, and we forget about ourselves. So each day we have to find ourselves through a deep meditation, and this I have learned to get it through Transcendental Meditation, which is a very simple practice. It takes only 20 minutes in the morning and 20 minutes in the afternoon—or any time of the day where you can be in silence with yourself—without making any big efforts to try, and to dispel all the tensions, all the preoccupations which you accumulate during the day. Then you re-regulate yourselves, and then you can now know how to care about the others.[9]

Unquestionably, in furthering peace in a war-torn country, President Joaquin Chissano increased the chance for his people's happiness in a way that might otherwise not have happened. But what about Cambodia, a country 8,367 kilometers (5,200 miles) away from Mozambique that shared its plunge into war and catastrophe? What is Cambodia's story?

Chapter 20

Cambodia

Heyam Duhkham Anāgatam
Avert the danger before it arises

Patanjali's Yoga Sūtra[1]

Cambodia's relatively recent history is one of tragedy and renewal. The tragedy was the buildup of a negative influence in collective consciousness that created the brutal regime of the Khmer Rouge. The leader of the Khmer Rouge, Pol Pot, was a Marxist dictator determined to create an agrarian utopia through social engineering. Instead, he became the architect of a miserable regime that caused the deaths from execution, starvation, and abuse of around two million people. Between 1975 and 1979, Cambodia writhed under the "Cambodian genocide." But Pol Pot's attempts to extend his influence into neighboring Vietnam resulted in his downfall. The Vietnamese army invaded Cambodia (at the time renamed Kampuchea) and removed him and the Khmer Rouge from power. The Cambodian government was left in chaos and the country in extreme poverty, unhappiness, and grief at the loss of a precious generation.

The beginnings of renewal

In November 1978, an initiative to bring peace to Cambodia during the Khmer Rouge reign was included as part of the World Peace Project. It was the same peace initiative that brought a measure of calm to Zambia and Mozambique. The Cambodian initiative, however, started in Thailand when 200 practitioners of the Transcendental Meditation and TM-Sidhi program gathered near the Thailand-Cambodia border

147

with the aim of keeping the war from spreading to Thailand.[2] An additional aim was to create a positive influence in the collective consciousness of the region and bring peace and well-being to the heartbroken Cambodian people. Two months after the peace-creating group started its program at the Thai border with Cambodia, Pol Pot and the Khmer Rouge were overthrown.

Was the timing a coincidence or did the presence of a nearby peace-creating group impact Cambodia's collective consciousness? A two-month gap between the arrival of the group and the overthrow of Pol Pot is a longer time than is usual with the Maharishi Effect but given the terrible stress that was widespread in Cambodia at that time, it is not surprising if the impact on Cambodia's collective consciousness took longer than the norm. The precise mechanics of the Maharishi Effect are not fully understood, and the level of stress and tensions in the local collective consciousness is a factor that could easily delay the result. However, if it was not a coincidence, we can be forgiven for asking what would have happened in the next ten years if that group or a much larger group had been able to stay in Cambodia.

The following years were troubled indeed. In 1990, Cambodia was rife with political dissension, economic woes, and problems with antigovernment guerillas in the eastern part of the country. Then, in 1991, following three years of arduous negotiations, almost 20 long years of very uncivil war ended as Cambodia's four fighting factions at last signed a peace agreement. In 1992, the United Nations sent a large peacekeeping force to Cambodia, which no doubt helped to stabilize the country, but the UN mission came in for criticism from The East-West Center, a U.S. Government-funded think tank. In a report on the UN mission, UN personnel were accused of helping to introduce HIV into Cambodia.

Return of the King

In 1993, Cambodia became a monarchy again with the return of King Norodom Sihanouk. During the same year, a new university named Maharishi Vedic University (MVU) opened its doors to students. The aim of the university was to achieve educational excellence, carry out research to extend the frontiers of knowledge, and improve the quality of life for the nation. Achieving educational excellence is a great goal, but the aim of the new university extended far beyond this goal. The intention was to foster inner values of life such as peace, happiness, intelligence, and creativity, and in the process, increase harmony in Cambodia's collective consciousness.

The result was that beginning in 1994, more than 550 students from almost every Cambodian province practiced the Transcendental Meditation program together and 100–200 students practiced the TM-Sidhi program in a group. Hence, from 1993 to 2008, up to 1,250 students contributed to increased coherence in collective consciousness across three MVU campuses through their daily group practice of the Transcendental Meditation program, and became their own peace-creating group for the nation.[3] The university faculty included Cambodian and international professors with degrees from Australia, New Zealand, and elsewhere, and the project began in 1993 and unfortunately ended in 2008 when the University became the Chea Sim University of Kamchaymear (CSUK).

Cambodia was an extremely poor country in 1990, and the poorest of the world's 152 countries in the next few years. However, according to a recently published study, authored by Ken Cavanaugh, Michael Dillbeck, and David Orme-Johnson, Cambodia witnessed "a 6.0% annual rate of reduction in violence during the experimental period 1993–2008."[4] The data was provided by Virtual Research Associates, Inc., a commercial provider of news reports, unaware of the hypotheses of the study. Drs. Cavanaugh, Dillbeck, and Orme-Johnson concluded that the reduction in violence "could not plausibly be attributed to pre-existing trends, seasonal or other cycles in the data, or the activities of a UN peacekeeping mission that failed in its mission to disarm and demobilize the warring factions in the civil war."[5]

King Norodom Sihanouk of Cambodia is quoted as saying: "Maharishi Vedic University is playing an important role in human resource development and in [the] restoration of peace and expansion of prosperity throughout the country."[6] But it was not just increasing peace that drew a mention. One of the students stated that the education offered at Maharishi Vedic University helped "bestow on us physical, moral, mental and spiritual strength to plunge into the modern world."[7] These are qualities worth having in any nation.

A few more examples of peace creation are presented in the next chapter together with reasons for taking the Maharishi Effect very seriously indeed.

Chapter 21

Bringing Peace and Well-being?

Let the time come, as come it will, when the masses will realize that the true human successes are those which triumph over the mysteries of matter and of life. At that moment a decisive hour will sound for mankind, when the spirit of discovery absorbs all the momentum contained in the spirit of war.

Pierre Teilhard de Chardin[1]

Assessing a nation's quality of life is a way, albeit subjective, of measuring the nation's happiness level. If the nation is suffering from conflict and poverty, not much happiness can be expected. If it is peaceful and prosperous, we would expect its happiness level to be higher. Without wanting to over-repeat, the *Bhagavad Gītā* states that peace is the basis of happiness. Certainly, without peace, whether it is peace of mind or national peace, happiness will always carry with it an element of anxiety. That is not real and stable happiness.

Notwithstanding some notable deterioration in peacefulness in Greece and Austria, the European collective consciousness is doing well as Europe is still the most peaceful region in the world according to the 2021 Global Peace Index (GPI).[2] Ireland is a good example of a peaceful European state. At the time of writing, the Republic of Ireland has increased to #8 on the GPI ranking scale of 163 countries. Like other countries, Ireland experienced its share of anti-lockdown protests due to the recent pandemic, yet it is an increasingly peaceful nation and regarded as an increasingly happy nation. However, the prize for the world's most peaceful country still goes to Iceland for the 14th year running. This charming Nordic island possesses neither an army, a navy, nor an air force. What it does possess is an astonishingly low crime rate, an excellent education and welfare system, and a delightful sense of well-being. In other words, it is considered a happy country.

Uneasy peace

Unfortunately, as continued peace is fragile and needs to be nurtured, every country or continent needs to continually take steps to ensure it stays peaceful. As stated by the 2021 Global Peace Index, global peace has deteriorated for the ninth year in a row (although this deterioration is smaller than in some previous years). Unless the world's most intelligent people understand and maintain a positive global collective consciousness, conflict is never far away. In the past 20 years alone, a number of European crises have arisen: Serbia, Croatia, Kosovo, the Russian/Georgian war, and now the ongoing Russian/Ukrainian war. Hence, even largely peaceful Europe cannot sit back and sleep. Make no mistake: if collective consciousness is weak, then unhappiness, violence, conflict, and even war are like tigers waiting in the wings, ready to spring if the circumstances are right. The secret is to strengthen collective consciousness and keep it strong, and one way to maintain national well-being appears to be the Maharishi Effect.

It is not always easy to publish studies on unusual topics. The fact that there are so many published studies on the Maharishi Effect gives some indication of the effectiveness of the program and the rigor of the research. Some of these studies will be presented in this chapter. Please bear in mind that while the studies focus on reduced crime or conflict, they are also indications of a better quality of life, because higher levels of crime do not equate with higher levels of happiness any more than war equates with a high level of national well-being. Whatever feeling of justification may be present, commitment and even moments of joy will be accompanied by anxiety, and in the end, grief because people are killed and injured in war.

How many can feel satisfaction with life when they have to take numerous precautions to keep themselves, their families, and their possessions safe? We don't need a scientific study to tell us that happiness declines in areas of high crime. We see it in people's expressions, and we feel it in the collective atmosphere of such areas.

The U.S. 1972–1975

Building on previous small-scale studies, the first of their kind, an early study investigated changes in the crime rate of 24 U.S. cities between 1972 and 1977. The reason for choosing these particular cities was that in each one, 1% of the population had already started the Transcendental Meditation technique by 1972. To avoid any charge of bias, lead researcher Dr. Michael Dillbeck added a control group of 24 other cities under the independent eye of Mohan Shrestha of Bowling Green State University. Other factors that could have had an impact on crime rates were also taken into account, including the average level of education, unemployment rate, percentage of people under the poverty line, percentage living in the same residential area after five years, and per capita income.

For the five-year period before 1972 and the five-year period up until 1977, incidents of crime were assessed using publicly available data. Dr. Dillbeck's research indicated that once the 1% threshold was reached, a significant decrease in the crime rate occurred, averaging 22% in the 1% cities as compared with a 2% increase for the control cities (p<.001). In 1981, this study was published in the *Journal of Crime and Justice*.[3] It was the first study on the Maharishi Effect to be published and many more followed.

Rhode Island 1978

Rhode Island is located in the New England region of the United States, bordering Connecticut on the west and the

Atlantic Ocean on the south. It was once dominated by different Native American tribes but now is a thriving part of the U.S., known among other things for its silverware and beautiful jewelry. Back in the summer of 1978, however, it was the venue for a study named the Ideal Society Campaign. This was the first publicly announced, prospective (as opposed to retrospective) experimental study that researched the effects of a group practicing the TM and TM-Sidhi program together. This is what happened.

About 300 teachers of the TM program arrived in Rhode Island and began to teach Transcendental Meditation with the aim of instructing at least 1% of the Rhode Island population. Hence, at the beginning of that long ago August, 5,045 people had been instructed in the Transcendental Meditation program in 1978, and the 300 teachers were practicing Transcendental Meditation and the TM-Sidhi program together in groups in several cities in Rhode Island. The combination of more than 5,000 practicing TM and the 300 practicing the TM-Sidhi program was enough to create coherence for the one million population at the time of the study.[4]

The results were assessed using time series analysis for seven years of monthly data beginning in 1974 and ending in 1980. The variables examined were the FBI total crime rate, motor vehicle fatality rate, motor vehicle accident rate, death rate, per capita beer consumption, per capita cigarette consumption, unemployment rate, and degree of pollution. Researchers Michael Dillbeck and his team then continued their evaluation for a further two years as the possibility that the quality of life may have improved anyway in that part of the United States had to be considered. And so, the team contrasted what was happening in Rhode Island with neighboring demographically matched Delaware. The results were significant. Time series analysis found that the quality of life in Rhode Island did indeed improve ($p<.01$) in terms of a decrease in deaths, crime, auto accidents, motor vehicle fatalities, unemployment, pollution, and alcoholic beverage and cigarette consumption.

Improvements also continued after the group left the state, most probably due to the increased number of meditators. But because the meditators and practitioners of the TM-Sidhi program were no longer together in large groups, the improvements were less. The results of this study were also published in *The Journal of Mind and Behavior*.[5]

The Philippines

The Philippines consists of an archipelago of beautiful islands; its people are of Indigenous, Spanish, or mixed heritage, and the archipelago itself has a turbulent history of invasions and conflicts. Martial law had been imposed in 1972 and violence was rife. Nevertheless, in 1979, 400 employees of a resident business enterprise became a peace-creating group, practicing the Transcendental Meditation and TM-Sidhi program together in the morning and in the evening. The square root of 1% for the Philippines was approximately 400 at the time so the group was just big enough to have an impact on the quality of life. Combining the most reliable statistics on crime, fetal deaths, and other deaths into a Quality-of-Life Index, researchers conducted a study focusing on monthly data for Metro Manila and the Philippines. When the numbers in the group were at their height, the quality of life improved in the Philippines in terms of reduced crime, fetal deaths, and other mortality rates.

Regrettably, as the group size declined, so did the effect. This research was also included in *The Journal of Mind and Behavior*, as were studies on the effect of creating more coherence through the Maharishi Effect in Puerto Rico and New Delhi.[6] The editor of *The Journal of Mind and Behavior* gave several reasons for deciding to publish, as this next quote indicates, and the quote was included in the same publication.

The theory being proposed was a complete departure from the norm in either psychology or sociology, but this was a study well done. The statistical evidence was persuasive. What I had to consider is that judging new ideas in any scientific field is an extremely delicate task. On the one hand, you never want to propound errors. On the other hand, you need to keep the field open for innovation and progress. I'm afraid that many times, new ideas don't lose out on their merits. They lose out because established people in the field don't want to see their power eroded by new ideas which threaten their expertise and authority. In any event, Michael Dillbeck [the author of the study] had written a strong paper with solid evidence. I didn't see how I could deny that paper publication.[7]

Lebanon 1982–1984

The Lebanese civil war was brutal, long, and complex. The country lost approximately 200,000 people and much of its infrastructure. Shi'a Muslims fought Sunni Muslims, and Greek Orthodox Christians fought Maronite Christians. Amid all the fighting and terrible insecurity, Baskinta, a small Lebanese village seated at the foot of Mount Sannine, became the focus for further research on the Maharishi Effect.

Inspired by five previous studies, neuroscientist Tony Nader decided to discover whether his native home, the village of Baskinta, could find peace within the chaos of war. Dr. Nader and his team made a bold prediction: if 1% of Baskinta's 10,000-strong population learned the Transcendental Meditation technique, fewer casualties, less shelling, and reduced property damage would follow. Sure enough, this is exactly what happened. Teachers of Transcendental Meditation arrived and began to teach the Transcendental Meditation program to as many people as they could, and in July 1982, the 1% threshold was reached. (Five even learned the TM-Sidhi program.) The researchers did not rest but immediately began to examine the death and injury rate, the number of grenades and mortars fired at Baskinta, and any property damage. The Lebanese newspapers *Al Nahar* and *Al Amal*, plus the radio station, the *Voice of Lebanon*, were the sources of the data. True to form, the Maharishi Effect acted as a kind of armor for the town. Once 1% of Baskinta's population (100 participants) had learned Transcendental Meditation, the media reported that the shelling of Baskinta ceased completely, no one was killed or injured, and the buildings stood.[8]

This was an intriguing study, but no more so than the study that took place in Israel.

Israel 1983

The origin of conflicts is always complicated, and nowhere more complicated than the Israeli/Lebanon conflict. In fact, the origins are too complex to discuss in depth here. But in summary, the former prime minister of Israel, Menachem Begin, was determined to defeat the Palestinian Liberation Front (PLO); the Palestinian Liberation Front was determined not to be defeated; Begin ordered the Israeli air force to bomb PLO strongholds; the PLO retaliated by attacking Israel's northern border towns; and Israel launched an invasion into southern Lebanon. A brief history certainly, but the depressing reality is that in 1983, Israel was in a state of high tension. So, when a group of researchers predicted to an independent review board that a peace-creating group in Jerusalem would result in an improved quality of life in Jerusalem as measured by reduced car accidents, fires, and crime, and the same peace-creating group would improve the quality of life for Israel as a whole as measured by decreased crime, improved national mood, and reduced war deaths in Lebanon, curiosity was rampant.

A non-belligerence agreement had been signed between Israel and Lebanon in May 1983, but Israeli troops had not yet completely withdrawn from Lebanon. Then, in August 1983, researchers set up a peace-creating group in Jerusalem and called it the International Peace Project in the Middle East (IPPME). The goal of the IPPME was "to generate continuous group practice of the Transcendental Meditation and TM-Sidhi program for two months in East Jerusalem."[9] The numbers attending varied but were enough to have an effect. Here are some of the results:

- Israeli withdrawal: Two weeks of continuous high numbers in the peace-creating group peaked on Saturday, September 3, the same date as the long-awaited Israeli withdrawal from the Shouf region of Lebanon to a Southern Security zone. The Israelis could have withdrawn on any date, but they withdrew at the exact moment the group numbers in Jerusalem were at their highest.
- Crime decreased in Jerusalem and Israel
- Fires and car accidents also decreased in Jerusalem
- The index of quality of life rose in Israel and Jerusalem
- The fierceness of conflict between Israel and Lebanon diminished
- War fatalities in Lebanon decreased as predicted.

This research was published in the *Journal of Conflict Resolution* in 1988 and demonstrated the strength of the Maharishi Effect. It was a prospective study that assessed the Maharishi Effect across diverse climactic, political, and military conditions, and it was rigorous and powerful enough to be published in one of the most prestigious journals of conflict resolution at the time.[10] In fact, research studies on the Maharishi Effect have been published in *Social Indicators Research*; *The Journal of Mind and Behavior*; the *Journal of Crime and Justice*; *SAGE Open Journal*; *Psychology, Crime & Law*; *Journal of Offender Rehabilitation*; *Journal of Conflict Resolution*; and the *Journal of Social Behavior and Personality*.[11] This is not an insignificant list for a new phenomenon indicating that individual consciousness impacts collective consciousness and can improve the quality of life in terms of the well-being, and by inference, the happiness of the population.

A further examination

The Maharishi Effect was tested further when researchers John Davies and Charles Alexander investigated seven peace-creating assemblies where participants practiced the Transcendental Meditation and TM-Sidhi programs in groups theoretically large enough to impact the fighting in war-torn Lebanon. The dates and countries are shown below.

- August 1983 Israel
- December 1983 USA
- March 1984 Lebanon itself
- July 1984 former Yugoslavia
- July 1984 USA
- December 1984 The Netherlands
- July 1985 USA

Each assembly was arranged many weeks before starting and voiced its aim in advance: reduce violence with the Maharishi Effect. To analyze changes in the war, the researchers appointed an independent expert in media content analysis. The expert was aware of the politics and the cultural context of the war, and collected daily statistics on war deaths, injuries, and overall fighting from a number of leading international news sources. The expert was also not permitted to know the purpose of the study, the predicted changes, assembly dates, or the theory and technology behind the hypothesis.[12] The data indicated that during the 93 days (compared with 728 control days) that the numbers in the assemblies were high and capable of impacting the war in Lebanon, the results were staggering.

- War deaths dropped by 71%
- War injuries dropped by 68%
- Armed conflict dropped by 48%
- Cooperation among antagonists increased by 66%.[13]

In addition, the study controlled for other factors that might have had an influence on Lebanon, including seasonal cycles, temperature changes, prior trends in the war, bias toward the Maharishi Effect, media coverage, etc., but none of these could account for the changes. The positive effects created by the peace-creating groups began almost as soon as each group reached the requisite threshold, confirming the original hypothesis that the Maharishi Effect would influence the collective consciousness if the numbers reached the square root of 1%. Sadly, when the groups dispersed, the positive effects broke down, but, after an extraordinarily long delay, the study was eventually published in 2005 in the *Journal of Social Behavior and Personality*.[14] Why it took so long to be published is the topic of another book.

Washington D.C. 1993

The National Demonstration Project to Reduce Violent Crime and Improve Governmental Effectiveness in Washington D.C., taking place in the summer of 1993, was a well-publicized demonstration of the power of the Maharishi Effect. The Demonstration Project brought 4,000 practitioners of the TM and TM-Sidhi program to Washington D.C., with the stated goal of reducing crime and improving quality of life, and with specific predicted outcomes lodged in advance with governmental officials. The story goes like this. Earlier that year, in March, a major snowstorm hit the U.S., causing many deaths, and dropping about 14 inches of snow on Washington D.C. This storm, nicknamed the Storm of the Century, was likely to have been in the mind of a Washington policeman who quipped that it would take two feet of snow to reduce crime in D.C. that summer. This is saying a great deal because summers in Washington tend to be hot, and crime, with some exceptions, typically increases in hot temperatures. But in June and July 1993, crime actually dropped as the numbers participating in the National Demonstration Project reached its peak.[15] To add credibility to the study, the FBI crime data was supplied by a District of Columbia Metropolitan Police Department statistician who was also one of the co-authors, and the data was compiled by the Roper Institute for Public Opinion Research from a variety of polling organizations.[16]

Results from the demonstration project suggest that when the numbers reached four thousand in the final week, a reduction in the crime rate, increased media positivity toward the president, and improved congressional bipartisanship took place, all of which were predicted to the independent review board in advance.

There are many factors that may contribute to the speed of results. These include the size of the overall population, which in Washington D.C. that year was estimated at 3,539,000; the genetic similarity of the practitioners and the population, bearing in mind that the U.S. capital is international; and the quality of experiences of Transcendental Consciousness during Transcendental Meditation practice. Unsurprisingly, the overall factor appears to be that the more stressed the area, the more numbers may be needed to have an effect. So how does a nation create a group large enough to impact the entire nation on a permanent basis?

A university of peace

In Fairfield, Iowa, a university exists that was originally founded in Santa Barbara in 1971. Maharishi International University (MIU) is the world's flagship institution of Consciousness-Based[SM] education, where all fields of academic study are taught in the light of the development of consciousness.

Accredited by the Higher Learning Commission through the Ph.D. level, MIU provides both in-depth academic knowledge and the opportunity for students to unfold their full inner potential through daily practice of Transcendental Meditation and its advanced programs. Consequently, the university prizes the development of individual and societal consciousness. Students, staff, and faculty are encouraged to practice the Transcendental Meditation technique and its advanced programs, and brain patterns and higher states of consciousness are researched through its Center for Brain, Cognition, and Consciousness.

Over the years, MIU has hosted thousands of practitioners of the Transcendental Meditation and TM-Sidhi programs, many of whom practice these programs together with the goal of improving the quality of life in the U.S. From time to time, the size of this group has been large enough to create a demonstrable effect of peace in society. For instance, between 1982 and 1985, when the group size exceeded the predicted threshold needed to produce measurable change (the square root of 1% of the U.S. population), car accidents, suicides, and homicides decreased substantially across the country.[17] Results were equally as significant when an even larger group assembled at MIU from 2007–2011. This group consisted of practitioners of the TM-Sidhi program supplemented by a substantial group of Indian experts in Vedic knowledge.

Four studies on the effects of this larger group were published in 2016 and 2017.

While the chart on the following page may resemble several tangled strings, it does show something extraordinary. Let me explain. Over the four years examined by the studies (2007–2011), the average numbers practicing the Transcendental Meditation and TM-Sidhi program in the group were near or above the necessary threshold of 1,792. Drs. Michael Dillbeck and Kenneth Cavanaugh were the authors of the first study, which focused on two variables: the rate of homicides and violent crime in 206 urban areas. Dillbeck and Cavanaugh found a statistically significant decrease in violent crime and homicide rates during the study period and suggested that 8,157 homicides may have been averted during those four years.[18]

Figure 4. Results of the field effect of consciousness.

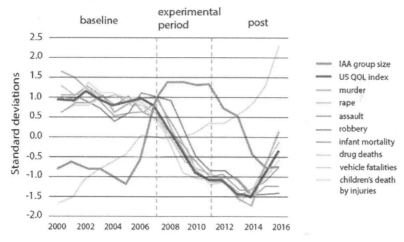

IAA Group Size and US Quality of Life Indices

Orme-Johnson, D.W., Cavanaugh, K.L., & Dillbeck, M.C. (2020). Field effects of consciousness: The Influence of Group Practice of Transcendental Meditation and the TM-Sidhi Programme on the US Quality of Life 2000 to 2016. *The Journal of social change, in preparation.*

The second study analyzed only homicide rates in the same 206 cities and recorded a 28.4% drop in the homicide rate, greater in fact than in the rest of the U.S.[19] The third study demonstrated a 20.6% reduction of the U.S. motor vehicle fatality rate and a 13.5% reduction of other accidental deaths between 2007 and 2010 due to group practice of the Transcendental Meditation and TM-Sidhi program in Fairfield.[20] And the fourth study showed a 30.4% decrease in drug-related fatalities (both pharmaceutical and illegal drugs) and a 12.5% decline in infant mortalities during the same period.[21] And all this through a peace-creating group located in a thriving university in Iowa intent on creating a happier world.

Latest studies

Two more studies on the Maharishi Effect were published in 2022. The first was published in July in *Studies in Asian Social Science*, an international peer-reviewed and open-access journal that publishes research in all areas of Asian social science. This study begins by pointing out that Western contemporary scientific theories of consciousness, in general, assume that consciousness is private to each individual and no shared consciousness, or collective consciousness, exists. The authors of the study refute this and propose an "interpersonal, nonlocalized dimension of consciousness that underlies and influences both individual consciousness, or individual mind, and the 'collective consciousness' of society."[22] The non-localized dimension of consciousness is, of course, Transcendental Consciousness, the source of both individual and collective consciousness.

The study's authors review previous research on the Maharishi Effect in Cambodia, the Philippines, and other countries, and present new findings demonstrating the existence of collective consciousness, its influence on trends in society, and the positive impact of Transcendental Meditation and its advanced programs on collective consciousness. The latest study, however, published in December 2022 in the *World Journal of Social Science*, enlarges the July study. In fact, it is the longest and most comprehensive study to demonstrate the significance of group practice of Transcendental Meditation and the TM-Sidhi program on U.S. national stress.

Unlike previous studies, the researchers explain that the aim of the 17-year study was to test the hypothesis that U.S. national stress would increase when the size of the coherence creating group declined. The study replicates and extends the results of five previous papers, and "consolidates all the variables studied in those papers into one analysis so their individual dynamics can be viewed together."[23] The results of the study indicate that the field effects of consciousness are profound, that national stress decreased significantly during the period of the study, and that collective consciousness became far more positive. When participation in the study was at its peak, indicators of stress such as homicides, rape, aggravated assault, robbery, infant mortality, drug-related deaths, motor vehicle fatalities, fatalities due to injuries in youths ages 10–19, all decreased. When the size of the group decreased over the next five years, sadly, indicators of stress increased. These results could not be explained by economic conditions, political leadership, population demographics, or policing strategies prevalent at the time.[24]

Lead researcher David Orme-Johnson explains:

What is unique about this study is that the results are so visually striking and on such a large scale. We see reduced stress on multiple indicators at the predicted time for the entire United States over a five-year period. And when the size of the group declined, national stress began increasing again. Clearly, the group was causing the effect.[25]

These concepts are not easy to explain. But then, descriptions of a law of nature sometimes precede theory, a prime example being gravity. English mathematician and physicist Sir Isaac Newton developed a theory of gravity that is more of a description than an explanation. He described a law but did not suggest how something could cross from one mass to another and exert a force.[26] It was not until Albert Einstein explained gravity as a curvature in space-time itself, and that changes in the curvature transmit "like a wave at the speed of light," that a fuller, but not complete, understanding of gravity was provided.[27] Before Einstein, the understanding was: "This is how it is. We don't understand the theory, but the law holds true," or to put it in a nutshell, theory is an explanation while law is a description.

What does all this mean? It means that every time the crime rate decreases as in the U.S. between 2007 and 2011, or every time war deaths are averted as in Baskinta in 1982, tension eases and we can walk down a street with less fear. We can bring up our children with less anxiety for their future, we can sit in a garden and not be afraid that a missile will fall, we can experience Transcendental Consciousness during meditation without disruption, and we can experience greater peace and happiness. That is what it means.

Chapter 22

Repeating the Dose

One day we must come to see that peace is not merely a distant goal we seek, but that it is a means by which we arrive at that goal.

Martin Luther King[1]

Today, it is not enough to say, "This is how it is" and expect scientists to simply accept the proffered theory. Scientists have come to expect more and rightly so. In my previous book, *An Antidote to Violence: Evaluating the Evidence*, sixteen reasons for having confidence in the Maharishi Effect were given, but for *Creating a Happy World*, only a few of those reasons have been selected. The first is possibly the most important; replication, replication, replication.

In evaluating whether research is genuine or not, the most important question is "Can it be repeated?" In the case of the Maharishi Effect, the constant replication of results has confirmed its validity. Studies have replicated the effect under different conditions, at different times of the year, or have broken down one large study into smaller studies. The Maharishi Effect has been widely demonstrated in regions ranging from the U.S. to the Philippines, from Europe and the U.K. to Cambodia, and from Israel to Lebanon. In addition, studies have measured the Maharishi Effect in summer, spring, fall, and winter, and the long-term U.S. study mentioned in the previous chapter, lasting continuously through all four seasons.

Endorsements

Allowing an experiment to be replicated by independent researchers is another way of ensuring impartiality. This kind of replication is more likely to happen when one paper is published and then another researcher weighs in to see if similar results can be obtained. At the present time, 21 peer-reviewed studies and 50 demonstrations of the Maharishi Effect have been conducted by different researchers, not all of them associated with the Transcendental Meditation organization. Consider the following endorsements of the Maharishi Effect. Two of them are from practitioners of the Transcendental Meditation technique. The others are not. It is worth adding that not every TM practitioner is biased in favor of the Maharishi Effect and not every non-TM individual is biased against it.

I have been following the research on Maharishi's [approach to peace] as it has developed over the last twenty years. There is now a strong and coherent body of evidence showing that (this approach) provides a simple and cost-effective solution to many of the social problems we face today. This research and its conclusions are so strong, that it demands action from those responsible for government policy.

Huw Dixon, Professor of Economics at Cardiff University, Wales[2]

I think the claim can be plausibly made that the potential impact of this research exceeds that of any other ongoing social or psychological research program. It has survived a broader array of statistical tests than most research in the field of conflict resolution. This work and the theory that informs it deserve the most serious consideration by academics and policy makers alike.

David Edwards, Ph.D., Professor of Government, University of Texas at Austin[3]

...the hypothesis seems logically derived from the initial premises, and its empirical testing seems competently executed. These are the standards to which manuscripts submitted for publication in this journal are normally subjected. The manuscript, either in its initial version or as revised, was read by four referees (two more than is typical with this journal): three psychologists and a political scientist.

Bruce Russett, editor, *Journal of Conflict Resolution*[4]

...both the level of exposition and the application of statistical methods for hypothesis testing are commensurate with this reviewer's standards of scientific research ... clearly our literature is large enough to absorb competing schools of thought on various issues.

Robert Duval, *Journal of Conflict Resolution*[5]

I was initially skeptical, but having studied the research completed to date, I have concluded that these studies on the [Maharishi Effect] have subjected theory to proper empirical tests. They have shown sound results that demand serious interest. This method should be applied more widely in programs to reduce crime.

Ken Pease, formerly Professor of Criminology at the University of Huddersfield and a member of the British Home Office National Crime Prevention Board 1993–6[6]

The possibility is that we have made one of the most important discoveries of our time.

Dr. Juan Pascual-Leone, Professor Emeritus at York University in Ottawa, Canada[7]

In response to those who might say that the majority of research has been carried out by individuals who are most interested in the Maharishi Effect, I am happy to point them toward a paper by Norman Lederman, Professor of Mathematics and Science Education at the Illinois Institute of Technology, and

Fouad Abd-El-Khalick, Professor and Dean of the School of Education at the University of North Carolina at Chapel Hill. In this paper, the authors state:

Too many students and teachers believe that scientific knowledge is provable in an absolute sense, objective, and devoid of creativity and human imagination. It is also just as common for students and teachers to believe that laws are theories that have been proven and that there exists a single step-wise scientific method which characterizes scientific investigations.[8]

There is not just one way to establish the truth of a phenomenon. Scientists view knowledge and the path to gaining reliable knowledge through the lens of their common framework of perception, the theories that provide scientists with their basic beliefs, concepts, and methodology. Even the way that objects of observation are interpreted is due to this framework, or paradigm. Indeed, the very concept of what is considered to be "objective" depends on inter-subjective agreement, meaning agreement between many people within the paradigm of a common perception. A past example of this was the commonly held view of classical physics that objects were solid and "real." This viewpoint changed radically with the advent of quantum physics, which demonstrated that atoms consist of whirlpools of energy that constantly spin and vibrate, and what was considered solid is in fact nothing but energy. Moreover, a different example of subjective knowledge and learning is given by Dr. Tony Nader, who states:

Art also expresses emotions, feelings, imagination, and the inner sense of order and harmony. It satisfies the senses, and by making concrete the abstract realms of life, gives a tangible reference to the mind about aesthetics, order, and harmony.

Certain forms of art also appeal to the intellect. The intricate symmetries and constructs in architecture and in classical music, for example, sometimes entice an intellectual analysis that helps reveal their beauty. As knowledge has organising power, intellectual understanding of certain aspects of art awakens a greater appreciation for them. Some aspects of art evoke feelings and emotions, while depicting and expressing intimate aspects of inner life. For this reason, art has been also used for worship, and as a way to teach, to train, to elevate the spirit, and inspire goodness and courage.

Art therefore can also be seen as a form of subjective knowledge. It is a physical expression of abstract realities. It depicts feelings; it depicts the shape and sound of the Transcendent, the mind and the feelings. Its harmony is the harmony of the inner being; its shape is the shape of the mind; its sound is the sound of the silently vibrant Self.[9]

This is supported by the American artist Robert Henri, who, in 1923, wrote in his book *The Art Spirit*:

There are moments in our lives, and there are moments in our day when we seem to go beyond the usual. Such are the moments of our greatest happiness. Such are the moments of our greatest wisdom. If one could but recall his vision by some sort of sign. It was in this hope that the arts were invented. Signposts on the way to what may be. Signposts toward greater knowledge.[10]

Self-experimentation

For scientists researching as yet unexplained phenomena, the only way forward may sometimes be through systematic inquiry and self-experimentation since, at present, other credible forms of experimentation that can lead to a full understanding of the phenomenon may not exist. Fortunately, the contribution of self-experimentation throughout the last few centuries has been considerable. Sir Isaac Newton attempted to understand visual hallucinations by staring at the sun. The 19th century psychologist Hermann Ebbinghaus broke new ground with the experimental study of memory, and the late Seth Roberts, emeritus professor of psychology at the University of California, Berkeley, stated that self-tracking, a frequent investigative tool on the Internet, is "the future of self-experimentation."[11]

The dosage effect

The dosage effect is yet another factor that can be considered consistent with a causal hypothesis for the Maharishi Effect. Dosage in the case of the Maharishi Effect is a simple formula; the more people who practice Transcendental Meditation, the more likelihood there is of peace, and for two years between October 1981 and October 1983, this formula was demonstrated. As more people participated in the Transcendental Meditation and TM-Sidhi program at the College of Natural Law in Washington D.C., the more violent crime declined. Neither changes in police coverage nor neighborhood watch programs could explain the results, nor could other variables such as per capita income, the density of the population and average years of education, the weather, political events, or how many young people aged between 15–29 made up the population.[12]

Breaking down one large experiment into smaller experiments took place in the IPPME study, which aimed for 200 participants but had to settle for a fluctuating number that varied between 65 and 241. Nevertheless, the crucial factor was that the influence of the group could now be evaluated according to the changing numbers. Four attendance quartiles emerged: 65–124, 125–157, 158–179, and 180–241, permitting the authors of the study to compare the different periods. With the higher numbers (more than 197), "only 9.7 people died on average each day in the Lebanon conflict. When the group was less than 124, an average of 40.1 people died each day."[13] This was the tragic reality. The higher the numbers, the fewer the deaths. The lower the numbers, the greater the deaths. In this case, the study confirmed the efficacy of the Maharishi Effect but recorded the inevitable pain of death and grieving relatives when the numbers were lower. If we could only create a happier world, the records would not be able to document so many deaths.

Studies on the Maharishi Effect are quasi-experiments; increases in the number of practitioners in the large groups precede the reductions in crime and violence, not the other way around; studies meet the highest standard of social research; they control for alternative theories and demonstrate that results are not due to seasonal changes or trends; and they are tested through time series analysis, Cross-Lagged Analysis methods, the LISREL Covariance Structural Model, linear transfer function analysis, and the Akaike Information Criterion. With results and built-in safeguards against spurious results such as these, it is very hard to dismiss the Maharishi Effect. It is based on experiences of the omnipresent field of Transcendental Consciousness, and since this field can be accessed by practitioners of the Transcendental Meditation and TM-Sidhi techniques, then it should be possible to create a field effect and create a better quality of life.

Verification for this assertion comes from observation of the Maharishi Effect. To date, over 50 demonstrations and over 20 studies published in peer-reviewed journals confirm that large groups of TM and TM-Sidhi practitioners consistently create this field effect throughout society, transforming social trends in a positive and meaningful direction and thereby demonstrating the existence of an underlying field of consciousness. The Maharishi Effect does not replace other means to create peace.

It simply enables peace-creating organizations everywhere to be more effective. Enlivenment of the field of Transcendental Consciousness in collective consciousness softens the atmosphere and thereby creates the ground for more positivity, peace, and happiness in society and the world.

Chapter 23

Final Thoughts

The soul of the world is nourished by people's happiness.

Paolo Coelho[1]

There are three overall premises in this book. First, that the source of peace and happiness lies in the experience of a deep underlying consciousness, referred to as Transcendental Consciousness, pure consciousness, the Tao, or the Self. Second, that Transcendental Meditation can help people rise to a better state of peace, happiness, and fulfillment if we are open to experiencing it—and that the benefits of this rise can be scientifically verified. Third, that a similar rise to a better state of peace, happiness, and fulfillment can take effect in society through the positive influence on collective consciousness generated by practitioners of Transcendental Meditation and its advanced programs. This influence too can be measured.

The question "where do we go from here" can be left up to readers. It seems from various reports that the world's happiness level is not in a particularly good place at present. Nevertheless, that situation can change, and it will change faster if collective consciousness is understood, if more people experience Transcendental Consciousness, and if the Maharishi Effect is permanently created on different continents so that it can support the work of all peace-creating organizations.

According to the American Academy of Arts and Sciences (AAAS), public confidence in scientific leaders has remained relatively stable over the past 30 years, public investment in science is strongly supported, and the majority of Americans view scientific research as beneficial.[2] But it seems from the AAAS report that although the majority of people trust science, they also form their own opinions about research findings and applications. A recent survey from *ScienceCounts* indicated that two-thirds of people assumed that a COVID vaccine labeled as "safe" would carry a risk of side effects. Out of this group, 40% believed that only a small percentage would experience mild side effects, 15% expected that the side effects would be common, and 13% expected that the side effects would be severe for a small number of people. Yet, most did not reject the science behind the vaccine.

What this means is that since science and scientists are largely trusted by the public, scientific institutions could do more to encourage further research on the Transcendental Meditation program, collective consciousness, and the Maharishi Effect. As far as the Maharishi Effect research is concerned, a remark by sociologist Mark Novak is telling: "The repeated effect is very persuasive. You might discount it once or twice, but seven times gets your attention."[3] As research and the experiences of people around the world have shown, it seems that individual happiness is bound up with developing human consciousness beyond what is understood today, and the happiness of a society is bound up with the strength of the Maharishi Effect, which depends on the collective influence of those practicing the Transcendental Meditation technique and its advanced programs.

Finding peace

If we look for tranquility, it will be found at the source of our thoughts and feelings. By practicing Transcendental Meditation and its advanced programs morning and evening, we can develop higher states of consciousness and eventually reach the supreme pinnacle of fulfillment in Brahman Consciousness. Imagine a world where everyone was either in Brahman Consciousness or approaching it. The level of peace and happiness would be beyond imagination, and even the thought of a small portion of that happiness would be a welcome relief from all the sadness and suffering that still seems to be part of our world. Can we achieve the glory of a world where, according to the Rām Charit Mānasa, every river flows with an abundance of refreshing water, cool, pure, and delicious to the taste? Where the sea remains within its bounds, casting forth pearls on its shore for all to gather? Maybe we can ... in time. But we can certainly create a world of far greater happiness than we have now. I leave the last words to Maharishi Mahesh Yogi, who knew infinite happiness.

> Brahman is the Reality which embraces both the relative and absolute fields of life. Having gained the state of Brahman, a man has risen to the ultimate Reality of existence. In this state of enlightenment he has accomplished eternal liberation, and once a man has risen to this state there is no falling away from it.[4]

Brahman is infinite joy.

Citations and Notes

Introduction

1. Hume, D. The Stoic, *Essays, Moral, Political and Literary*, part 1, essay 16, in *The Philosophical Works of David Hume* (1826), volume 3, 167.
2. Helliwell, J.F., Layard, R., Sachs, J.D., De Neve, J.E., Aknin, L.B. & Wang, S. (Eds.). (2022). World Happiness Report 2022. New York: Sustainable Development Solutions Network.

Chapter 1

1. Rām Charit Mānasa, Uttara Kāṇd 20.1–4; 22.1–4; 23.1. Translated by Thomas Egenes, Ph.D.
2. Ibid. 20.
3. Gallup: World. 28 June 2022. World Unhappier, More Stressed Out Than Ever, by Julie Ray.
4. Helliwell, J.F., Layard, R., Sachs, J.D., De Neve, J.E., Aknin, L.B. & Wang, S. (Eds.). (2022). World Happiness Report 2022. New York: Sustainable Development Solutions Network.
5. World Health Organization. 28 September 2022. WHO and ILO call for new measures to tackle mental health issues at work. Joint News release. Geneva, Switzerland.
6. The Mayo Clinic. Depression (major depressive disorder) - Symptoms and causes - Mayo Clinic.
7. World Health Organization. 13 September 2021. Depression (who.int).
8. UNICEF 2021. The State of the World's Children 2021 | UNICEF.
9. *The Guardian*. 9 April 2018. 'Social media has poisoned us': young Britons on why they are unhappy | Young people | *The Guardian*.

10. Yakult. 13 August 2019. Yakult wants to help young people find their purpose - ShelfLife magazine.
11. Suicide increasing amongst Europe's youth. 18 January 2022. Suicide increasing amongst Europe's youth, governments underprepared – EURACTIV.com.
12. Ibid. World Happiness Report 2022.
13. https://wgntv.com/news/chicago-news/woman-who-collapsed-downtown-meets-good-samaritan-who-helped-save-her/
14. https://www.fox4news.com/news/off-duty-dallas-officer-saves-woman-after-fiery-crash
15. https://www.wsbtv.com/news/trending/hurricane-ian-good-samaritan-helps-locate-84-year-old-woman-stranded-rising-waters/KRUNRBQNONGN5BESRKQRQLIFVU/

Chapter 2

1. Reik, T. (1957). *A Psychologist Looks at Love*, chapter 3, 194.
2. Lyubomirsky, S., Sheldon, K.M., Schkade, D. (2005). Pursuing Happiness: The architecture of sustainable change. *Review of General Psychology*, Volume 9, No. 2, 111–131.
3. What is Epigenetics? Centers for Disease Control and Presentation. What is Epigenetics? | CDC.
4. Travis, F.T. (2012). *Your Brain Is a River, Not a Rock*, 38.
5. Lyubomirsky, S., King, L., Diener, E. (2005). The Benefits of Frequent Positive Affect: Does Happiness Lead to Success? *Psychological Bulletin*, 2005, Volume 131, No. 6, 803–855.
6. Warrenburg, S. (2005). *Chemical Senses*, Volume 30, Issue suppl_1, January 2005, pp. i248–i249, https://doi.org/10.1093/chemse/bjh208
7. Warrenburg, S. (2002). Measurement of Emotion in Olfactory Research. In Given, P. and Paredes, D. (Eds.), *Chemistry of Taste: Mechanisms, Behaviors, and Mimics*. American Chemical Society, Washington, D.C., 243–260.

8. Warrenburg, S. (2004). Effects of Fragrance on Emotions: Moods and Physiology. *Chemical Senses*, Volume 30, Issue suppl_1 January 2005, pp. i248–i249, https://doi.org/10.1093/chemse/bjh208

9. Daumann, J., Wagner, D., Heekeren, K., Neukirch, A., Thiel, C.M. (2010). Neuronal correlates of visual and auditory alertness in the DMT and ketamine model of psychosis. *J. Psychopharmacol.* 24, 1515–1524.

10. Barker, S.A. (2018). N, N-Dimethyltryptamine (DMT), an Endogenous Hallucinogen: Past, Present, and Future Research to Determine Its Role and Function. *Front Neurosci.* 2018 August 6;12:536. doi:10.3389/fnins.2018.00536. PMID: 30127713; PMCID: PMC6088236.

11. Ayahuasca: Overview, Uses, Side Effects, Precautions, Interactions, Dosing and Reviews (webmd.com). Retrieved 11 September 2022.

12. Malcolm, B.J., Lee, K.C. (2017). *Ayahuasca*: An ancient sacrament for treatment of contemporary psychiatric illness? *Ment Health Clin.* 2018;7(1):39–45. Published 2018 March 23. doi:10.9740/mhc.2017.01.039.

13. Travis, T. (2022). Relation between Psychedelic and Transcendental Experiences. *International Journal of Psychological Studies*, Volume 14, No. 4; 2022 ISSN 1918-7211 E-ISSN 18-722X.

14. Ibid.

15. Ibid.

Chapter 3

1. Nabokov, V. (1981). Philistines and Philistinism, *Lectures on Russian Literature*.

2. Kifer, Y., Heller, D., Perunovic, W., Galinsky, A. (2013). The Good Life of the Powerful: The Experience of Power and Authenticity Enhances Subjective Well-Being. *Psychological Science*, Volume 24.

3. Wood, A.M., Linley, P.A., Maltby, J., Baliousis, M. & Joseph, S. (2008). The Authentic Personality: A Theoretical and Empirical Conceptualization and the Development of the Authenticity Scale. *Journal of Counseling Psychology*, 55 (3), 385–399. https://doi.org/10.1037/0022-0167.55.3.385

4. Sutton, A. (2020). Living the good life: A meta-analysis of authenticity, well-being and engagement. *Personality and Individual Differences*, 153. doi:10.1016/j.paid.2019.109645

5. Kifer et al.: Ibid.

Chapter 4

1. Seneca the Younger. (1917). *Moral Letters*, R. Gummere, trans.

2. Waldinger, R. (2015). What makes a good life? Lessons from the longest study on happiness | TED Talk.

3. Steger, M.F., Kashdan, T.B., Oishi, S. (2008). Being good by doing good: Daily eudaimonic activity and well-being. *Journal of Research in Personality*, Volume 42, Issue 1, 2008, 22–42.

4. Ibid.

5. Aristotle. *Nicomachean Ethics* (p. 6). Veritatis Splendor Publications. Kindle Edition.

6. Ibid. 8.

7. Plato. *The Republic* (Coterie Classics) (p. 40). Penguin Classics. Kindle Edition.

8. Ibid. 41.

9. Ibid. 85–86.

10. Maharishi Mahesh Yogi. (1990). *Maharishi Mahesh Yogi on the Bhagavad-Gītā: A new translation and commentary*, Chapters 1–6. Arkana, Penguin Books (Original work printed in 1967), 61–62.

11. Maslow, A.H. *Toward a Psychology of Being* (p. 67). Start Publishing LLC. Kindle Edition.

12. Ibid. 148.

13. Ibid. 145.
14. de Jager Meezenbroek, E., Garssen, B., van den Berg, M. et al. (2012). Measuring Spirituality as a Universal Human Experience: A Review of Spirituality Questionnaires. *J Relig Health* 51, 336–354 (2012). https://doi.org/10.1007/s10943-010-9376-1
15. Ryff, Carol D. Eudaimonic Well-Being, Inequality, and Health: Recent Findings and Future Directions. *International Review of Economics*, volume 64, no. 2, 30 March 2017, pp. 159–178, doi:10.1007/s12232-017-0277-4

Chapter 5

1. David Lynch Foundation. (2022). A message from General James "Spider" Marks. The Resilient Warrior Program (resilient-warriors.org).
2. Scott, E. (2020). How to Enjoy a Chocolate Meditation (verywellmind.com).
3. Rosenthal, Norman. *Transcendence* (pp. 94–95). Penguin Publishing Group. Kindle Edition.
4. Mission statement of the David Lynch Foundation (DLF). About DLF (davidlynchfoundation.org).
5. Personal communication.
6. Spivack, B., Saunders, P. (2020). *An Antidote to Violence: Evaluating the Evidence.* Changemakers Books, 56–57.
7. Lutz, A., Slagter, H.A., Dunne, J.D., Davidson, R.J. (2008). Attention regulation and monitoring in meditation. *Trends Cogn Sci.* Apr;12(4):163-9. doi: 10.1016/j.tics.2008.01.005. Epub 2008 March 10. PMID: 18329323; PMCID: PMC2693206.
8. Travis, F. & Shear, J. (2010). Focused attention, open monitoring and automatic self-transcending: categories to organise meditations from Vedic, Buddhist and Chinese traditions. *Consciousness and Cognition*, 19(4), 3.
9. Travis, F. & Shear, J. (2010). Ibid.
10. Travis, F. & Shear, J. (2010). Ibid.

11. Zhao, S., Uono, S., Li, C., Yoshimura, S. & Toichi, M. (2017). The Influence of Self-Referential Processing on Attentional Orienting in Frontoparietal Networks. *Frontiers in Human Neuroscience.* https://doi.org/10.3389/fnhum.2018.00199

12. Travis, F. and Parim, N. (2017). Default Mode Network Activation and Transcendental Meditation Practice: Focused Attention or Automatic Self-Transcending? *Brain and Cognition*, 111:86-94.

13. Personal communication, S.K.

14. Personal communication, M.Y.

15. Ellis, G. *A Symphony of Silence: An Enlightened Vision*, 2nd Edition. CreateSpace Independent Publishing Platform. Kindle Edition.

16. Ibid.

17. Prisons in Norway: Inside a Norwegian Jail (lifeinnorway.net).

Chapter 6

1. Tolkien, J.R.R. *The Lord of the Rings*, Illustrated (p. 88), (*The Fellowship of the Ring*). Harper Collins. Kindle Edition.

2. Kohn, A. (2017). Do We Perform Better Under Pressure? | *Psychology Today*.

3. Maharishi brings to light the relationship between happiness and bliss when he states, "bliss is omnipresent and eternal, while happiness is the expression of the reflection of the omnipresent bliss on the mind." In referring to the bliss that can be experienced with deep experiences of the transcendent, he explains that it is "fullness of life, perfection of existence, and therefore completely unattached to anything in the relative field, completely free from the influence of action."

4. MacLean, C.R.K., Walton, K.G., Wenneberg, S.R. et al. (1997). Effects of the transcendental meditation program on adaptive mechanisms: Changes in hormone levels and responses to stress after 4 months of practice.

Psychoneuroendocrinology, 1997;22(4):277-295. doi:10.1016/ S0306-4530(97)00003-6

5. Yuen, H.K. & Jenkins, G.R. (2020). Factors associated with changes in subjective well-being immediately after urban park visit. *International Journal of Environmental Health Research*, 30:2, 134-145. DOI:10.1080/09603123.2019.1577368

6. American Heart Association: Pets and Heart Health: Dignity Health | Pets and Heart Health.

7. Transcendental Meditation May Improve Cardiac Risk Factors in Patients with Coronary Heart Disease. Cited on the David Lynch Foundation website. American Medical Association - David Lynch Foundation UK, June 12, 2006.

8. Bokhari, S., Schneider, R.H., Salerno, J.W. et al. Effects of cardiac rehabilitation with and without meditation on myocardial blood flow using quantitative positron emission tomography: A pilot study. *Journal of Nuclear Cardiology*: Official Publication of the American Society of Nuclear Cardiology. 2021 Aug;28(4):1596-1607. DOI: 10.1007/s12350-019-01884-9. PMID: 31529385; PMCID: PMC9178923.

9. Wallace, R.K., Marcus, J.B., Clark, C.S. (2020). *The Coherence Effect: Tapping into the Laws of Nature that Govern Health, Happiness, and Higher Brain Functioning*. Armin Lear Press, 115.

10. David Lynch Foundation's Center for Resilience. Transcendental Meditation for Veterans and Military Personnel (davidlynchfoundation.org).

11. Valosek, L., Link, J., Mills, P., Konrad, A., Rainforth, M., Nidich, S. (2018). Effect of meditation on emotional intelligence and perceived stress in the workplace: A randomized controlled study. *The Permanente Journal*, 22:17-172. DOI: https://doi.org/10.7812/TPP/17-172

12. Ibid.

13. *All Love Flows to the Self*. (1999). Eds. Kumuda Reddy & Thomas Egenes. Samhita Productions, 16.

Chapter 7

1. Maharishi Mahesh Yogi. (2019). *Science of Being and Art of Living* (15). MUM Press. Kindle Edition, 29.
2. Shakespeare, W. *Hamlet*, act 1, scene 3.
3. Maharishi Mahesh Yogi. (1990). *Science of Being and Art of Living* (27). MUM Press. Kindle Edition.
4. Maharishi Mahesh Yogi. (1990). *Maharishi Mahesh Yogi on the Bhagavad-Gītā: A new translation and commentary*, Chapters 1–6. Arkana, Penguin Books (Original work printed in 1967), 126.
5. Ibid. 127–131.
6. Ibid. 127–131.
7. Lao Tzu. *Tao Te Ching* (14). Ancient Renewal. Kindle Edition.
8. Ibid. 16.
9. Maharishi Mahesh Yogi. (2001). *Science of Being and Art of Living*. Plume Publications (Original work printed in 1963), 15.
10. Lao Tzu. *Tao Te Ching* (32). Ancient Renewal. Kindle Edition.
11. Ibid. 7.
12. Frances Hodgson Burnett. *The Secret Garden*. Delhi Open Books. Kindle Edition, Chapter 27.

Chapter 8

1. Jeans, J. (1930). *The Mysterious Universe*. Kindle Edition, p. 154.
2. Cartwright, D.E. *Schopenhauer* (p. 182). Cambridge University Press. Kindle Edition.
3. Nṛisiṃhottaratāpanīya Upanishad, 7.
4. Bartlett, G. (2018). Why Physicalism is Wrong | Issue 126 | *Philosophy Now*.
5. Physicalism (Stanford Encyclopedia of Philosophy).
6. *The Illusion of Consciousness*. Daniel Dennett. TED talk. 2003.

7. Bartlett, G. (2018). Why Physicalism is Wrong | Issue 126 | *Philosophy Now.*
8. René Descartes. *Meditations on First Philosophy* (p. 8). E-Bookarama. Kindle Edition.
9. Descartes: Ibid. 6.
10. Descartes: Ibid. 9.
11. Nye, A. (1999). *The Princess and the Philosopher. Letters of Elisabeth of the Palatine to René Descartes.* Rowman and Littlefield Publishers Inc., 9.
12. Kastrup, Bernardo. (2014). *Why Materialism Is Baloney: How true skeptics know there is no death and fathom answers to life, the universe, and everything* (pp. 8–9). John Hunt Publishing. Kindle Edition, 56.
13. Ibid. 9.
14. Ibid. 14.
15. Goff, P. *Galileo's Error.* Knopf Doubleday Publishing Group. Kindle Edition, Chapter 2 (Is There a Ghost in the Machine?).
16. Ibid. Chapter 5 (Consciousness and the Meaning of Life).
17. Ibid. Chapter 5 (Consciousness and the Meaning of Life).
18. Ibid. Chapter 5 (Consciousness and the Meaning of Life).

Chapter 9

1. Henry, R. The Mental Universe. *Nature* 436, 29 (2005). https://doi.org/10.1038/436029a
2. Joye, S. (2020). *David Bohm's Implicate Order: New Frontiers in the Evolution of Consciousness* (21). Kindle Edition.
3. Dyson, F. (1988). *US News and World Report,* 72.
4. Planck, M. (25 January 1931). *The Observer,* London.
5. Vernon, M. (2012). It's Time for Science to move on from Materialism. *The Guardian* newspaper. January 28.
6. Jeans, J. (1930). *The Mysterious Universe.* Kindle Edition, p. 154.
7. Ibid. 150.

8. Hagelin, J. (2019). *Foundations of Physics and Consciousness*. Maharishi International University Press, 12.2.
9. Ibid. 12.2.
10. Spivack, B., Saunders, P. (2020). *An Antidote to Violence: Evaluating the Evidence*. Changemakers Books, 99.
11. Tononi, G. (2008). Consciousness as integrated information: A provisional manifesto. *Biol. Bull* 215: 216–242.
12. Travis, F.T. (2020). Consciousness is Primary: Science of Consciousness for the 21st Century. *International Journal of Psychological Studies* 13(1):1 DOI:10.5539/ijps.v13n1p1
13. Travis, F.T. (2005). The Significance of Transcendental Consciousness for Addressing the "Hard" Problem of Consciousness. *Journal of Social Behavior and Personality* 17, 123-135.

Chapter 10

1. Hagelin, J. (1998). *Manual for a Perfect Government*. Maharishi International University Press.
2. Nader, P.T.M. (2015). *International Journal of Mathematics and Consciousness*, Volume 1, Number 1. Maharishi International University Press.
3. Nader, P.T.M. (2021), *One Unbounded Ocean of Consciousness in Motion*. AGUILAR. Kindle Edition, 18.
4. Ibid. 7.
5. Ibid. 11.
6. Ibid. 11.
7. Nader, P.T.M. (2015). *International Journal of Mathematics and Consciousness,* Volume 1, Number 1. Maharishi International University Press.
8. *Vasistha's Yoga*. (1993). Swami Venkatesananda. State University of New York Press.
9. Ibid. 278.
10. Lao Tzu. *Tao Te Ching* (42). Ancient Renewal. Kindle Edition.

11. The term "Shankarāchārya" refers to heads of monasteries called Mathas in the Advaita Vedānta tradition.
12. Maharishi Mahesh Yogi. (2001). *Science of Being and Art of Living*. Plume Publications (Original work printed in 1963), 3.

Chapter 11

1. Atrey, V. (2020). Random Forays: Raising the Levels of our Consciousness. Cited in *The Hindustan Times*. September 26.
2. Ramsay, L. (2021). NASA's Webb Will Join Forces with the Event Horizon Telescope to Reveal the Milky Way's Supermassive Black Hole. Nasa.gov. 27 October 2021. NASA Shares List of Cosmic Targets for Webb Telescope's First Images I NASA.
3. Scarpelli, S., Bartolacci, C., D'Atri, A., Gorgoni, M., De Gennaro, L. (2019). Mental Sleep Activity and Disturbing Dreams in the Lifespan. *Int J Environ Res Public Health*. 2019 Sep 29;16(19):3658. Doi: 10.3390/ijerph16193658. PMID: 31569467; PMCID:PMC6801786.
4. Maharishi Mahesh Yogi. (2019). *Science of Being and Art of Living* (p. 162). MUM Press. Kindle Edition.
5. Nader, P.T.M. (2000). *Human Physiology: Expression of Veda and the Vedic Literature*. Maharishi Vedic University Press, 135.
6. Maharishi Mahesh Yogi. (1995). *Maharishi Vedic University: Introduction*. Maharishi Vedic University Press, 58–59.
7. Larcher, V. (2015). Children are not small adults: Significance of biological and cognitive development in medical practice. *Handbook Philos Med*. doi:10.1007/978-94-017-8706- 2_16-1
8. Cherry, K. (2022). Jean Piaget: Life and Theory of Cognitive Development (verywellmind.com), 16 February.
9. Frances Hodgson Burnett. *The Secret Garden*. Delhi Open Books. Kindle Edition, Chapter 27.

10. Seton, Anya. *Katherine* (445). Harper Collins. Kindle Edition.
11. Hay, D. (2007). *Something There*. Templeton Press.
12. Maharishi Mahesh Yogi. (1978). *Enlightenment to every individual, invincibility to every nation*. Maharishi European Research University Press, 92.

Chapter 12

1. Gottfried Wilhelm Leibniz. (1965). *Philosophical Writings*. London: Dent, Rowman and Littlefield, 37 & 80.
2. Akhtar, N. (2022). Neurophysiology of Dreams. In: Gupta, R., Neubauer, D.N., Pandi-Perumal, S.R. (Eds.), *Sleep and Neuropsychiatric Disorders*. Singapore: Springer. https://doi.org/10.1007/978-981-16-0123-1_4
3. We have two amygdalae, located in the left and right temporal lobes and often referred to as the "fear center" of the brain. However, there is more to the amygdalae than that, as they are involved in many aspects of thought, behavior, and emotions.
4. Maharishi Mahesh Yogi. (2001). *Science of Being and Art of Living*. New York: Plume Publications, 262.
5. Maharishi Mahesh Yogi. (1977). *Creating an ideal society: a global undertaking*. Age of Enlightenment Press, 123.
6. Plato. *Symposium*, 210d–211b, translated by Michael Joyce; reprinted in *The Collected Dialogues of Plato*, edited by Edith Hamilton and Huntingdon Cairns. Princeton University Press (1973, 562).
   Cited in Shear, J. (1990). *The Inner Dimension: Philosophy and the Experience of Consciousness*. Peter Lang, 2.
7. Bohm, D., Krishnamurti, J. *The Limits of Thought* (6). Taylor and Francis. Kindle Edition.
8. Pearson, C. (2016). *The Supreme Awakening: Experiences of Enlightenment Throughout Time — And How You Can Cultivate Them*. Organic Pears Press. Kindle Edition, Chapter 4.

9. Shankaracharya. *The Crest-Jewel of Wisdom* (50). Kindle Edition.
10. Spivack, B., Saunders, P. (2020). *An Antidote to Violence: Evaluating the Evidence*. Changemakers Books, 104.
11. Lao Tzu. *Tao Te Ching* (34). Ancient Renewal. Kindle Edition.
12. Otto, R. (1932). *Mysticism East and West*. New York: Macmillan, 61.
13. Alfred Lord Tennyson. (1885). *Tiresias and other Poems*. (The Ancient Sage.) Macmillan and Co., 67–68.
14. Cartwright, D.E. *Schopenhauer* (183). Cambridge University Press. Kindle Edition.
15. Cartwright: Ibid. 183.
16. Maharishi Mahesh Yogi. (1990). *Maharishi Mahesh Yogi on the Bhagavad-Gītā: A new translation and commentary*, Chapters 1–6. Arkana, Penguin Books (Original work printed in 1967), 136.
17. Katz, V., Egenes, T. (2015). *The Upanishads, A New Translation*. Tarcher Cornerstone Editions, 17.
18. Spivack, B., Saunders, P. (2020). *An Antidote to Violence: Evaluating the Evidence*. Changemakers Books, 58.
19. Travis, F. (2013). Advances in meditation research: Neuroscience and clinical applications. *Annals of the New York Academy of Sciences*, 1307, 1–8.

Chapter 13

1. Emerson, R.W., Thoreau, H.D. *Self-Reliance and Other Essays: With Walden*. Titan Read. Kindle Edition. (The Over Soul.)
2. Maharishi Mahesh Yogi. (1990). *Maharishi Mahesh Yogi on the Bhagavad-Gītā: A new translation and commentary*, Chapters 1–6. Arkana, Penguin Books (Original work printed in 1967), 136–137.

3. Maharishi Mahesh Yogi. (2019). *Science of Being and Art of Living* (338). MUM Press. Kindle Edition.

4. Travis, F. (2013). Advances in meditation research: Neuroscience and clinical applications. *Annals of the New York Academy of Sciences*, 1307, 1–8.

5. Ibid.

6. Maharishi Mahesh Yogi. (1990). *Maharishi Mahesh Yogi on the Bhagavad-Gītā: A new translation and commentary*, Chapters 1–6. Arkana, Penguin Books (Original work printed in 1967), 424.

7. Mason, L.I., Orme-Johnson, D.W. (2010). Transcendental Consciousness wakes up in dreaming and deep sleep. *International Journal of Dream Research*, 3(1):28–32.

8. Orme-Johnson, D.W. & Edwards, C. (1982). *Subjective experiences of stabilized pure consciousness*. Unpublished manuscript, Department of Psychology, Maharishi International University.

9. Travis, F. (1994). The junction point model: A field model of waking, sleeping, and dreaming relating dream witnessing, the waking/sleeping transition, and Transcendental Meditation in terms of a common psychophysiologic state. *Dreaming*, Volume 4. DOI:10.1037/h0094404.

10. Sullivan, J.W.N. *Beethoven—His Spiritual Development* (127). Read Books Ltd. Kindle Edition.

11. Montague, M.P. *Twenty Minutes of Reality: An Experience. With Some Illuminating Letters Concerning It.* Kindle Edition.

12. Maharishi Mahesh Yogi. (2001). *Science of Being and Art of Living* New York: Plume Publications, 246.

13. Maharishi Mahesh Yogi. (1990). *Maharishi Mahesh Yogi on the Bhagavad-Gītā: A new translation and commentary*, Chapters 1–6. Arkana, Penguin Books (Original work printed in 1967), 307.

14. Ibid. 359.

15. Nader, P.T.M. (2000). *Human Physiology: Expression of Veda and the Vedic Literature*. Maharishi Vedic University Press, 135.

16. Spivack, B., Saunders, P. (2020). *An Antidote to Violence: Evaluating the Evidence*. Changemakers Books, 121.

17. Cited in Pearson, C. (2016). *The Supreme Awakening: Experiences of Enlightenment Throughout Time—And How You Can Cultivate Them*. Organic Pears Press. Kindle Edition, Chapter 7.

18. Katz, V. (2011). *Conversations With Maharishi: Maharishi Mahesh Yogi Speaks about the Full Development of Human Consciousness*. Volume 1. Maharishi International University Press, 50–51.

19. Maharishi Mahesh Yogi. (2010). *The Flow of Consciousness: Maharishi Mahesh Yogi on Literature and Language, 1971 to 1976*. Edited by Rhoda F. Orme-Johnson, and Susan K. Andersen. Maharishi International University Press, 114–115.

Chapter 14

1. Ṛk Veda 1.164.46.

2. When Scientists "Discover" What Indigenous People Have Known For Centuries | Science | *Smithsonian Magazine*. 21 February 2018.

3. Sands, W.F. (2012). *Maharishi Mahesh Yogi And His Gift To The World*. Maharishi International University Press, 101.

4. Maharishi Mahesh Yogi. (1977). *Creating an ideal society: a global undertaking*. West Germany: MERU Press, 46.

5. An experience while practicing Transcendental Meditation by an anonymous participant during a long meditation retreat. Cited in *Invincible America Assembly: Experiences of Higher States of Consciousness of Course Participants*. Maharishi University of Management Press, 22.

6.   Maharishi Mahesh Yogi. (1990). *Maharishi Mahesh Yogi on the Bhagavad-Gītā: A new translation and commentary*, Chapters 1–6. Arkana, Penguin Books (Original work printed in 1967), 136.

7.   Maharishi Mahesh Yogi. (2019). *Science of Being and Art of Living* (338). MUM Press. Kindle Edition.

8.   Pearson, Craig. *The Supreme Awakening: Experiences of Enlightenment Throughout Time—And How You Can Cultivate Them*. Organic Pears Press. Kindle Edition.

9.   Maharishi Mahesh Yogi. (1990). *Maharishi Mahesh Yogi on the Bhagavad-Gītā: A new translation and commentary*, Chapters 1–6. Arkana, Penguin Books (Original work printed in 1967), 307.

10. Pearson, C. (2016). *The Supreme Awakening: Experiences of Enlightenment Throughout Time—And How You Can Cultivate Them*. Organic Pears Press. Kindle Edition, Chapter 6.

11. Ibid. Chapter 6.

12. An experience while practicing Transcendental Meditation by an anonymous participant during a long meditation retreat. Cited in *Invincible America Assembly: Experiences of Higher States of Consciousness of Course Participants*. Maharishi University of Management Press, 170.

13. Pearson, C. (2016). *The Supreme Awakening: Experiences of Enlightenment Throughout Time—And How You Can Cultivate Them*. Organic Pears Press. Kindle Edition, Chapter 6.

14. Lao Tzu. *Tao Te Ching*. Ancient Renewal. Kindle Edition, 22.

15. Pearson, C. (2016). *The Supreme Awakening: Experiences of Enlightenment Throughout Time—And How You Can Cultivate Them*. Organic Pears Press. Kindle Edition, Chapter 7.

16. An experience while practicing Transcendental Meditation by an anonymous participant during a long meditation retreat. Cited in *Invincible America Assembly: Experiences of Higher States of Consciousness of Course Participants*. Maharishi University of Management Press, 194.

Chapter 15

1. Martel, Y. (2002). *The Life of Pi*. Mariner Books.
2. Maharishi Mahesh Yogi. (1980). *Science, consciousness, and ageing: proceedings of the international conference.* Maharishi European Research University Press, 39.
3. Patanjali's Yoga Sūtra, 1.2; cited in Egenes, T., 2010, 11.
4. Sands, W.F. (2013). *Maharishi's Yoga: The Royal Path to Enlightenment.* Maharishi International University Press, 102.
5. The experience of a Ph.D. researcher at Maharishi International University.
6. Spivack, B., Saunders, P. (2020). *An Antidote to Violence: Evaluating the Evidence.* Changemakers Books, Chapter 14, 84. Endnote.
7. Maharishi Mahesh Yogi. (2001). *Science of Being and Art of Living.* New York: Plume Publications, 176.

Chapter 16

1. David Lynch Foundation. (2022). My Life is Back. Transcendental Meditation for Veterans and Military Personnel (davidlynchfoundation.org). (Operation Enduring Freedom, the official name of the U.S. Global War on Terrorism.)
2. Thutmose III was not only cultured, appreciating art and music, but also recognized the value of other cultures and was noteworthy in respecting human life (worldhistory.org/Thutmose III).
3. Mankoff, J. (2022). Russia's War in Ukraine: Identity, History, and Conflict. *Center for Strategic and International Studies* (csis.org.), https://www.csis.org/analysis/russias-war-ukraine-identity-history-and-conflict
4. Putin, V. (2022). On Break Up of USSR. Reported in *Reuters*. February 21, 2022. Extracts from Putin's speech on Ukraine I *Reuters*.

5. Clausewitz, Carl von. (2016). *On War*. Enhanced Media. First published 1873. Chapter 1.
6. *Bhagavad Gītā* 2.66.
7. Dalai Lama & Desmond Tutu, with Douglas Abrams. (2016). *The Book of Joy*. Penguin Random House, 14.
8. Thich Nhat Hanh. (2009). *The Art of Power*. HarperOne. Kindle Edition, 80.
9. Maharishi Mahesh Yogi. (1990). *Maharishi Mahesh Yogi on the Bhagavad-Gītā: A new translation and commentary*, Chapters 1–6. Arkana, Penguin Books (Original work printed in 1967), 214.
10. www.history.com.

Chapter 17

1. Maharishi Mahesh Yogi. (1978). *Enlightenment to every individual, invincibility to every nation*. West Germany: MERU Press, 47.
2. Global Union of Scientists for Peace (GUSP.org). (2022). David Lynch calls on Philanthropists to Create World Peace.
3. Durkheim, Émile. (2019). *The Division of Labor in Society* (87). Digireads.com Kindle Edition.
4. Ibid. 216.
5. Durkheim also asked whether it was true that "the happiness of the individual increases as man [humanity] advances?" And answers that he finds it doubtful (Ibid. 220).
6. Maharishi Mahesh Yogi. (1978). *Enlightenment to every individual, invincibility to every nation*. West Germany: MERU Press, 47.
7. Rich, A. (1969). *Music, Mirror of the Arts*. Praeger, 1st edition, 281.
8. Edmans, A., Fernandez-Perez, A., Garel, A., Indriawan, I. (2022). Music Sentiment and Stock Returns Around the

World. *Journal of Financial Economics*, Volume 145, Issue 2, Part A, Pages 234–254.

9. Combs, A., Krippner, S. (2008). Collective Consciousness and the Social Brain. *Journal of Consciousness Studies* 15(10–11):264–276.

10. What is Entanglement and Why is it Important? What Is Quantum Entanglement? Quantum Entanglement Explained in Simple Terms | Caltech Science Exchange.

11. Combs & Krippner: Ibid. (2008).

12. Sun Tzu. *The Art of War* (6). Neeland Media LLC. Kindle Edition.

13. Ibid. 24.

14. Ibid. 6.

15. Ibid. 30.

16. United Nations Biological Convention. Biological Weapons Convention – UNODA.

17. Conan-Doyle, A. *The Sign of the Four*. Chapter 1, p. 92; similar expressions occur in Chapter 6.

Chapter 18

1. 20 February 1896, *The Youth's Companion*, The Bar as a Profession (Part 2 of 2), by Mr. Justice Oliver Wendell Holmes (Supreme Judicial Court of Massachusetts), Start Page 92, Quote Page 92, Column 3, Perry Mason & Company, Boston, Massachusetts.

2. Maharishi Mahesh Yogi. (1986). *Thirty Years Around the World: Dawn of the Age of Enlightenment*. The Netherlands: Maharishi Vedic University Press, 430. Appearing first in *Tiroler Tageszeitung* (23 July 1962), Innsbruck, Austria.

3. Katz, V. (2011). *Conversations With Maharishi: Maharishi Mahesh Yogi Speaks about the Full Development of Human Consciousness*. Volume 1. Maharishi International University Press, 60.

4. Maharishi Mahesh Yogi. (1975). *Inauguration of the Dawn of the Age of Enlightenment*. MIU Press, 59.
5. Regrettably, this was a phenomenon that could, in pre-COVID days, more easily be put into practice. Today, people have an understandable tendency to shy away from groups.
6. Maharishi Mahesh Yogi. (1978). *Enlightenment to every individual, invincibility to every nation*. Maharishi European Research University Press, 258.
7. Spivack, B., Saunders, P. (2020). *An Antidote to Violence: Evaluating the Evidence*. Changemakers Books, 129.
8. Personal communication.
9. Personal communication.

Chapter 19
1. From an essay at Markkula Center for Applied Ethics, also quoted in *Architects of Peace: Visions of Hope in Words and Images* (2000), edited by Michael Collopy.
2. Spivack, B., Saunders, P. (2020). *An Antidote to Violence: Evaluating the Evidence*. Changemakers Books, 133–134.
3. The Mozambican Civil War (1977–1992) (blackpast.org.).
4. Astill, J. (22 September 2001). Meditation is path to peace, says Mozambique leader. *Guardian* newspaper. https://www.theguardian.com/world/2001/sep/22/jamesastill. Retrieved 6 June 2022.
5. Ibid.
6. Dai, T. (2011). Maharishi's formula for a prevention wing in the military — applied and found successful in Mozambique: case study 1993–1994, in R.S. Goodman & W.F. Sands (Eds.), *Consciousness-Based Education and Government*. Fairfield, IA: Maharishi University of Management Press, 453.
7. BBC News. Queen's Praise for Mozambique. 16 November 1999.

8. Lovell, J. (2007). Mozambique's Chissano wins Africa leadership prize. *Reuters*. 22 October 2007.

9. Gotabgaa Conference. (2010). A message from Joaquim Chissano, former President of Mozambique. *Institute for Excellence in Africa*. https://www.excellenceafrica.org/social-harmony-projects. Retrieved 10 January 2019.

Chapter 20

1. Patanjali's Yoga Sūtra, 2.16.

2. Dillbeck, M.C., Orme-Johnson, D.W. (1987). Physiological differences between Transcendental Meditation and rest. *American Psychologist*, 42(9):879–881.

3. Fergusson, L.C. & Cavanaugh, K.L. (2019). Socio-political violence in Cambodia between 1990 and 2008: An explanatory mixed methods study of social coherence. *Studies in Asian Social Science*, 6(2), 1–45.

4. Cavanaugh, K.L., Dillbeck, M.C. & Orme-Johnson, D.W. (2022). Evaluating a Field Theory of Consciousness and Social Change: Group Practice of Transcendental Meditation and Homicide Trends. *Studies in Asian Social Science*, 8(1), 1–32.

5. Ibid.

6. 23 May 2019. Group practice of Transcendental Meditation dramatically reduced violence in Cambodia, new study shows I EurekAlert!

7. Fergusson, L.C. & Bonshek, A.J. (2013). *Maharishi Vedic University in Cambodia: Educational Reconstruction and Social Renewal*. Gold Coast, Australia: Prana World Publishing, vi.

Chapter 21

1. Nelson, R.D. (2019). *Connected: The Emergence of Global Consciousness* (308). ICRL Press. Kindle Edition.

2. The Global Peace Index 2021. *The Global Peace Index 2021 Reveals a Year of Civil Unrest*. Institute for Economics and Peace.

3. Dillbeck, M.C., Landrith III, G.S. & Orme-Johnson, D.W. (1981). The Transcendental Meditation program and crime rate change in a sample of forty-eight cities. *Journal of Crime and Justice*, 4, 25–45.

4. Dillbeck, M.C., Cavanaugh, K.L., Glenn, T., Orme-Johnson, D.W. & Mittlefehldt, V. (1987). Consciousness as a Field: The Transcendental Meditation and TM-Sidhi Program and Changes in Social Indicators. *The Journal of Mind and Behavior*, 8(1), 67–103. http://www.jstor.org/stable/43853335

5. Ibid.

6. Ibid.

7. Ibid.

8. Nader, P.T.M., Alexander, C.N. & Davis, J.L. (1984). The Maharishi Technology of the Unified Field and reduction of armed conflict: A comparative, longitudinal study of Lebanese villages. *Scientific Research on Maharishi's Transcendental Meditation and TM-Sidhi Program: Collected Papers* (Volume 4, 2623–2633).

9. Spivack, B., Saunders, P. (2020). *An Antidote to Violence: Evaluating the Evidence*. Changemakers Books, 145.

10. Orme-Johnson, D.W., Alexander, C.N., Davies, J.L., Chandler, H.M. & Larimore, W.E. (1988). International Peace Project in the Middle East: The Effects of the Maharishi Technology of the Unified Field. *Journal of Conflict Resolution*, 32(4), 776–812.

11. Spivack, B., Saunders, P. (2020). *An Antidote to Violence: Evaluating the Evidence*. Changemakers Books, 36.

12. Pearson, C. (2008). *The Complete Book of Yogic Flying*. Fairfield, IA: Maharishi University Management Press, 537.

13. Ibid.

14. Davies, J.L. & Alexander, C.N. (2005). Alleviating political violence through reducing collective tension: impact assessment analyses of the Lebanon War. *Journal of Social Behavior and Personality*, 17(1), 304–5.
15. Hagelin, J.S., Rainforth, M.V., Orme-Johnson, D.W., Cavanaugh, K.L., Alexander, C.N., Shatkin, S.F., Davies, J.L., Hughes, A. & Ross, E. (1999). Effects of group practice of the Transcendental Meditation Program on preventing violent crime in Washington D.C.: results of the National Demonstration Project June–July 1993. *Social Indicators Research*, 47, 153–201.
16. Pearson, C. (2008). *The Complete Book of Yogic Flying*. Fairfield, IA: Maharishi University Management Press, 543.
17. Dillbeck, M.C. (1990). Test of a field theory of consciousness and social change: Time series analysis of participation in the TM-Sidhi program and reduction of violent death in the U.S. *Social Indicators Research* 22: 399–418.
18. Dillbeck, M.C. & Cavanaugh, K.L. (2016). Societal violence and collective consciousness: reduction of U.S. homicide and urban violent crime rates. *SAGE Open*, 6(2), 1–16. http://sgo.sagepub.com/content/6/2/2158244016637891
19. Cavanaugh, K.L. & Dillbeck, M.C. (2017A). Field effects of consciousness and reduction in U.S. urban murder rates: evaluation of a prospective quasi-experiment. *Journal of Health and Environmental Research*, 3(3–1), 34.
20. Cavanaugh, K.L. & Dillbeck, M.C. (2017B). The contribution of proposed field effects of consciousness to the prevention of US accidental fatalities: theory and empirical tests. *Journal of Consciousness Studies*, 24(1–2), 53–86.
21. Dillbeck, M.C. & Cavanaugh, K.L. (2017C). Group practice of the Transcendental Meditation and TM-Sidhi Program and reductions in infant mortality and drug-related death: a quasi-experimental analysis. *SAGE Open*, 7(1), 1–15. https://doi.org/10.1177/2158244017697164

22. Cavanaugh, K.L., Dillbeck, M.C. & Orme-Johnson, D.W. (2022). Evaluating a Field Theory of Consciousness and Social Change: Group Practice of Transcendental Meditation and Homicide Trends. *Studies in Asian Social Science*, 8(1), 1–32.

23. Orme-Johnson, D., Cavanaugh, K.L., Dillbeck, M.C., Goodman, R.S. (2022). Field-Effects of Consciousness: A Seventeen-Year Study of the Effects of Group Practice of the Transcendental Meditation and TM-Sidhi Programs on Reducing National Stress in the United States. *World Journal of Social Science* 9(2):1. https://scienmag.com/a-seventeen-year-landmark-study-finds-that-group-meditation-decreases-us-national-stress

24. Ibid.

25. Ibid.

26. Schurger, A. & Graziano, M.S.A. (2022). Consciousness explained or described? *Neuroscience of Consciousness*, 7, 1–9.

27. Ibid.

Chapter 22

1. Martin Luther King, Jr. (1965). Dreams of Brighter Tomorrows. *Ebony Magazine*. March.

2. *Global Peace Initiative*. http://globalpeaceproject.net/proven-results/endorsements/. Retrieved 13 January 2016.

3. Ibid.

4. Russett, B. (1988). *Journal of Conflict Resolution*, 32 (4), p. 773.

5. Duval, R. (1988). *Journal of Conflict Resolution*, 32 (4), pp. 813–814.

6. Brown, C.L. (1996). Observing the assessment of research information by peer reviewers, newspaper reporters, and potential governmental and non-governmental users: international peace project in the Middle East (unpublished doctoral dissertation). Cambridge, MA: Harvard University, 87.

7. Wallace, R.K. & Marcus, J.B. (2005). *Victory Before War*. Fairfield, IA: Maharishi University of Management Press, inside front cover.

8. Lederman, N.G. (1992). Students' and Teachers' Conceptions of the Nature of Science: A Review of the Research. *Journal of Research in Science Teaching*, 29, 331–359. https://doi.org/10.1002/tea.3660290404

9. Nader, T. (2000). *Human Physiology: Expression of Veda and Vedic Literature: Modern Science and Ancient Vedic Science Discover the Fabrics of Immortality in Human Physiology* (4th edition).

10. Henri, R. (1923). *The Art Spirit*. Innovative Books, p. 13.

11. Harrell, E. (2011). My Body, My Laboratory. *Time* magazine.

12. Hagelin, J.S., Rainforth, M.V., Orme-Johnson, D.W., Cavanaugh, K.L., Alexander, C.N., Shatkin, S.F., Davies, J.L., Hughes, A. & Ross, E. (1999). Effects of group practice of the Transcendental Meditation program on preventing violent crime in Washington D.C.: results of the National Demonstration Project June–July 1993. *Social Indicators Research*, 47, 153–201.

13. Spivack, B., Saunders, P. (2020). *An Antidote to Violence: Evaluating the Evidence*. Changemakers Books, 145.

Chapter 23

1. Coelho, P. (1988). *The Alchemist*. Harper Collins, 22.

2. American Academy of Arts and Sciences. (2018). Perceptions of Science in America.

3. Pearson, C. (2008). *The Complete Book of Yogic Flying*. Fairfield, IA: Maharishi University Management Press, 299.

4. Maharishi Mahesh Yogi. (1990). *Maharishi Mahesh Yogi on the Bhagavad-Gītā: A new translation and commentary*, Chapters 1–6. Arkana, Penguin Books (Original work printed in 1967), 291.

Author Biography

Patricia Saunders is a teacher of the Transcendental Meditation technique and taught Transcendental Meditation for many years in the U.K. Now, she is a teacher in the Consciousness and Human Potential department at Maharishi International University in Iowa. She has published many poems in online journals, and her nonfiction book, *An Antidote to Violence: Evaluating the Evidence,* was published in 2020 by Changemakers Books. It is now a bestselling book for Changemakers Books and John Hunt Publishing.

Thank you for purchasing *Creating a Happy World: Cultivating Happiness through the Transcendental Meditation Program.* My sincere hope is that you derived as much from reading this book as I did in writing it. If you have a few moments, please feel free to add your review of the book at your favorite online site for feedback.

O-BOOKS

SPIRITUALITY

O is a symbol of the world, of oneness and unity; this eye represents knowledge and insight. We publish titles on general spirituality and living a spiritual life. We aim to inform and help you on your own journey in this life.
If you have enjoyed this book, why not tell other readers by posting a review on your preferred book site?

Recent bestsellers from O-Books are:

Heart of Tantric Sex
Diana Richardson
Revealing Eastern secrets of deep love and intimacy to Western couples.
Paperback: 978-1-90381-637-0 ebook: 978-1-84694-637-0

Crystal Prescriptions
The A-Z guide to over 1,200 symptoms and their healing crystals Judy Hall
The first in the popular series of eight books, this handy little guide is packed as tight as a pill bottle with crystal remedies for ailments.
Paperback: 978-1-90504-740-6 ebook: 978-1-84694-629-5

Shine On
David Ditchfield and J S Jones
What if the aftereffects of a near-death experience were undeniable? What if a person could suddenly produce high-quality paintings of the afterlife, or if they acquired the ability to compose classical symphonies? Meet: David Ditchfield.
Paperback: 978-1-78904-365-5 ebook: 978-1-78904-366-2

The Way of Reiki
The Inner Teachings of Mikao Usui
Frans Stiene
The roadmap for deepening your understanding of the system of Reiki and rediscovering your True Self.
Paperback: 978-1-78535-665-0 ebook: 978-1-78535-744-2

You Are Not Your Thoughts
Frances Trussell
The journey to a mindful way of being, for those who want to truly know the power of mindfulness.
Paperback: 978-1-78535-816-6 ebook: 978-1-78535-817-3

The Mysteries of the Twelfth Astrological House
Fallen Angels
Carmen Turner-Schott, MSW, LISW
Everyone wants to know more about the most misunderstood house in astrology — the twelfth astrological house.
Paperback: 978-1-78099-343-0 ebook: 978-1-78099-344-7

WhatsApps from Heaven
Louise Hamlin
An account of a bereavement and the extraordinary
signs — including WhatsApps — that a retired
law lecturer received from her deceased husband.
Paperback: 978-1-78904-947-3 ebook: 978-1-78904-948-0

The Holistic Guide to Your Health
& Wellbeing Today
Oliver Rolfe
A holistic guide to improving your complete health,
both inside and out.
Paperback: 978-1-78535-392-5 ebook: 978-1-78535-393-2

Cool Sex
Diana Richardson and Wendy Doeleman
For deeply satisfying sex, the real secret is to reduce the heat,
to cool down. Discover the empowerment and fulfilment
of sex with loving mindfulness.
Paperback: 978-1-78904-351-8 ebook: 978-1-78904-352-5

Creating Real Happiness A to Z
Stephani Grace
Creating Real Happiness A to Z will help you understand
the truth that you are not your ego
(conditioned self).
Paperback: 978-1-78904-951-0 ebook: 978-1-78904-952-7

A Colourful Dose of Optimism
Jules Standish
It's time for us to look on the bright side, by boosting
our mood and lifting our spirit, both in
our interiors, as well as in our closet.
Paperback: 978-1-78904-927-5 ebook: 978-1-78904-928-2

Readers of ebooks can buy or view any of these bestsellers by
clicking on the live link in the title. Most titles are published
in paperback and as an ebook. Paperbacks are available in
traditional bookshops. Both print and ebook formats are
available online.

Find more titles and sign up to our readers' newsletter at
www.o-books.com

Follow O-Books on Facebook at **O-Books**

For video content, author interviews and more, please subscribe to our YouTube channel:

O-BOOKS Presents

Follow us on social media for book news, promotions and more:

Facebook: O-Books

Instagram: @o_books_mbs

Twitter: @obooks

Tik Tok: @ObooksMBS

www.o-books.com